Department of Economic and Social Affairs
Division for Sustainable Development

TRENDS

IN SUSTAINABLE DEVELOPMENT

Towards Sustainable Consumption and Production

United Nations
New York, 2010

DESA

The Department of Economic and Social Affairs of the United Nations Secretariat is a vital interface between global policies in the economic, social and environmental spheres and national action. The Department works in three main interlinked areas: (i) it compiles, generates and analyses a wide range of economic, social and environmental data and information on which Member States of the United Nations draw to review common problems and to take stock of policy options; (ii) it facilitates the negotiations of Member States in many intergovernmental bodies on joint courses of action to address ongoing or emerging global challenges; and (iii) it advises interested Governments on the ways and means of translating policy frameworks developed in United Nations conferences and summits into programmes at the country level and, through technical assistance, helps build national capacities.

Note

The designations employed and the presentation of the material in this publication do not imply the expression of any opinion whatsoever on the part of the Secretariat of the United Nations concerning the legal status of any country or territory or of its authorities, or concerning the delimitations of its frontiers. The term "country" as used in the text of the present report also refers, as appropriate, to territories or areas. The designations of country groups in the text and the tables are intended solely for statistical or analytical convenience and do not necessarily express a judgment about the stage reached by a particular country or area in the development process. Mention of the names of firms and commercial products does not imply the endorsement of the United Nations.

FOREWORD

The Johannesburg Plan of Implementation refers to sustainable consumption and production (SCP), along with poverty eradication and conservation of the natural resource base, as essential precondition for sustainable development. The idea of sustainable development contains within it the completion of three transitions: demographic, development, and decoupling. The demographic transition is at a mature stage and global population will level off around 9 billion later this century, and the share of urban population will expand briskly, especially in developing countries.

The development transition is far from complete. It refers to the time when the gains from development would reach all countries, and the consequent prosperity would be shared broadly. Currently, while the 15 per cent of the world's population that lives in developed countries has an average per capita income above $40,000, the 80 per cent in developing countries average income of less than $2,000 per capita. This is also reflected in the wide dispersion of human development indicators as well as per capita energy consumption.

The decoupling transition is also problematic. Already, the consumption patterns of the developed countries have imposed severe stresses on the earth's natural resources and largely filled its natural sinks. If the development transition were to follow the same consumption and production patterns, pressures on critical ecosystems and life-support systems would become intolerable. Thus, a key challenge facing the international community is how to sustain and even accelerate the development transition while also realizing the decoupling transition. An energy transition is also crucial, combining energy access for the poor with diffusion of renewable energy.

In short, we must find pathways which simultaneously achieve upward convergence of living standards (completing the development transition) and downward convergence of resource use and environmental impacts (the decoupling transition).

This volume reviews progress towards achieving these interlinked challenges, focusing first on broad trends in resource use, then turning to drivers of resource depletion and environmental degradation, and finally examining the major initiatives of governments, business and civil society to shift towards sustainable consumption and production patterns.

Tariq Banuri, Director
Division for Sustainable Development
Department of Economic and Social Affairs
April 2010

CONTENTS

I. TRENDS IN RESOURCE USE

In the past half century, per capita use of mineral resources, including fossil fuels, has been increasing steeply. Technological innovation that has improved material and energy efficiency has been overwhelmed by the sheer increase in demand from rising incomes and populations.

Population growth accelerated first before slowing during the 20th century, with world population exceeding 6 billion by 2000. The period since World War II has been marked by a historically unprecedented rise in living standards and levels of consumption experienced by a growing number of countries.

When broken down by region, industrialized countries, with 15% of the population, used 50% of the fossil energy, industrial minerals and metallic ores as of 2005. This is changing quickly, however. Between 1990 and 2006, total energy use in developing countries increased by 40% while in high-income OECD countries it increased by half as much.[1]

Much of the world's population remains poor and the gap in living standards between rich and poor needs to be narrowed substantially, not least to achieve the Millennium Development Goals (MDGs). The development transition needs to occur even as consumption and production patterns are transformed in a decoupling transition. Living standards of the poor must rise even as humankind's ecological footprint shrinks.

Consumers in developed countries and wealthy consumers everywhere will need to take the lead in moving towards sustainable patterns of consumption. Production systems also need to move towards sustainable patterns of resource use, with reduced pollution and waste. Developed country enterprises can chart the way forward, supporting their suppliers and partners around the world with technology and know how.

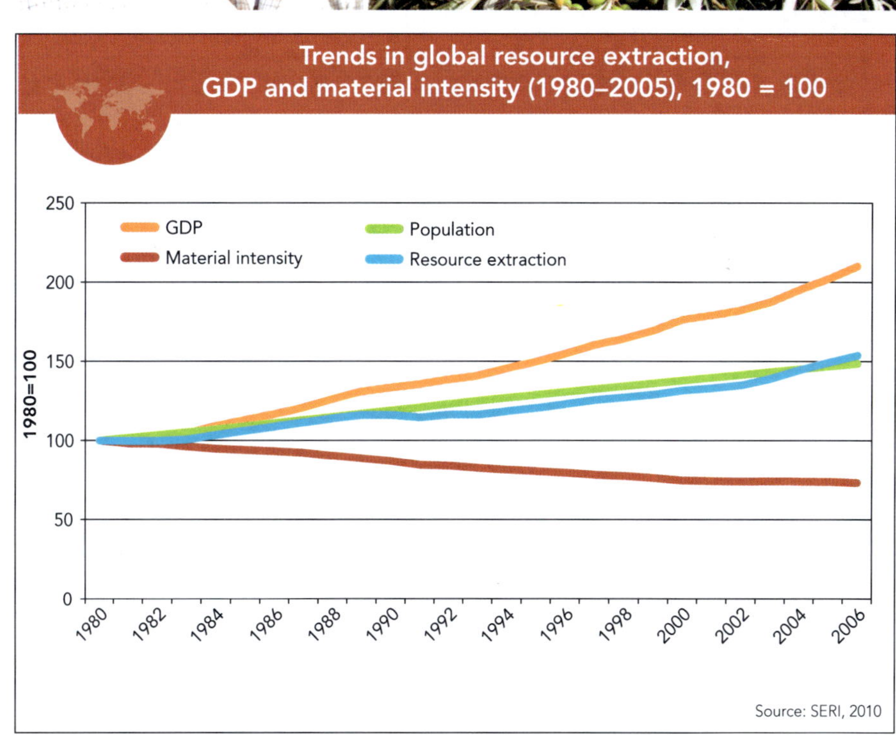

Trends in global resource extraction, GDP and material intensity (1980–2005), 1980 = 100

The accelerating materials and fossil energy demand of the past decade-and-a-half has begun to be reflected in commodity prices. Before the recent recession, most were spiraling upward. While a boon for resource-rich economies, the prices rises have been a bane for many resource- poor countries, which have been particularly hard it by high food prices.

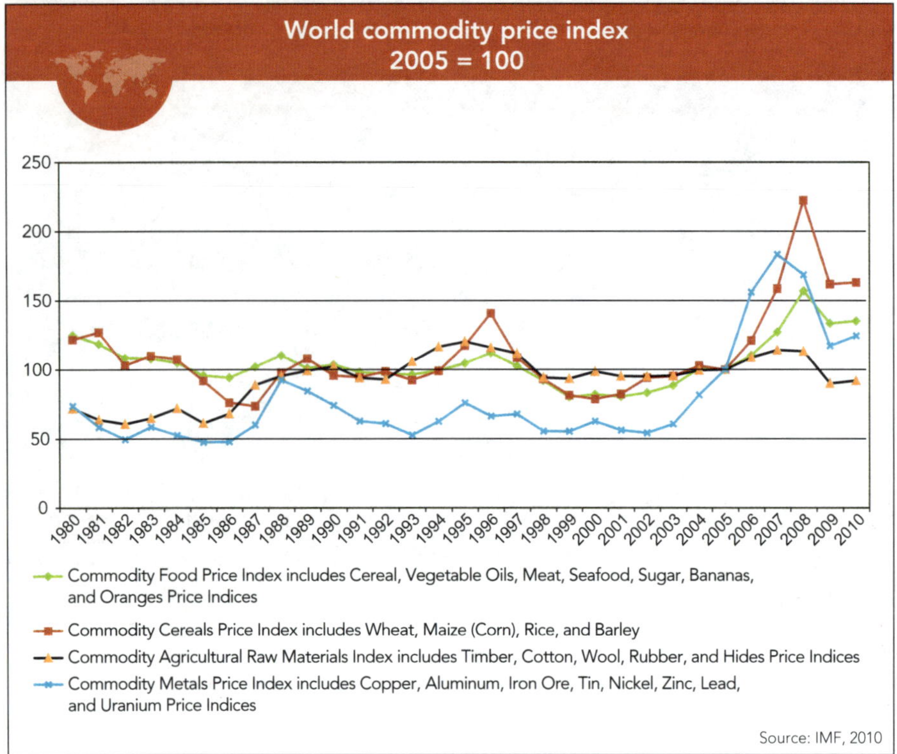

II. STRESSES ON ECOSYSTEMS

GENERAL TRENDS

Recent research published in the journal Nature defines, for eight earth bio-physical subsystems or processes, "safe" threshold boundaries that should not be exceeded to avoid major environmental disruptions. Already several thresholds appear to have been exceeded, including: climate change (as measured by excess CO_2 concentration in the atmosphere); the rate of bio-diversity loss (terrestrial and marine); and interference with the nitrogen cycle (N_2 is removed from the atmosphere and converted to reactive nitrogen for human use mainly for agriculture). Interference with the global phosphorous cycle, ocean acidification, global freshwater use, and change in land use are approaching their thresholds. No boundaries have yet been established for chemical pollution and atmospheric aerosol loading. Stratospheric ozone depletion is a noteworthy exception, where international environmental cooperation has yielded progress in reversing a negative trend.

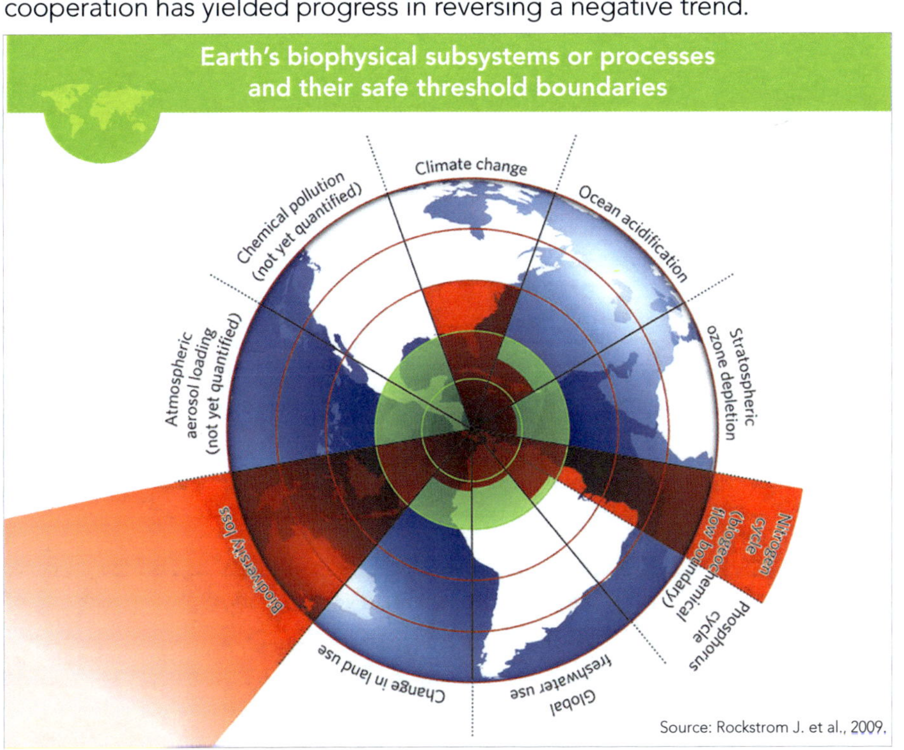

CLIMATE CHANGE

CO_2 emissions have been rising steadily: Since 1751 approximately 329 billion tons of carbon have been released to the atmosphere from the consumption of fossil fuels and cement production. Half of these emissions have occurred since the mid 1970s.

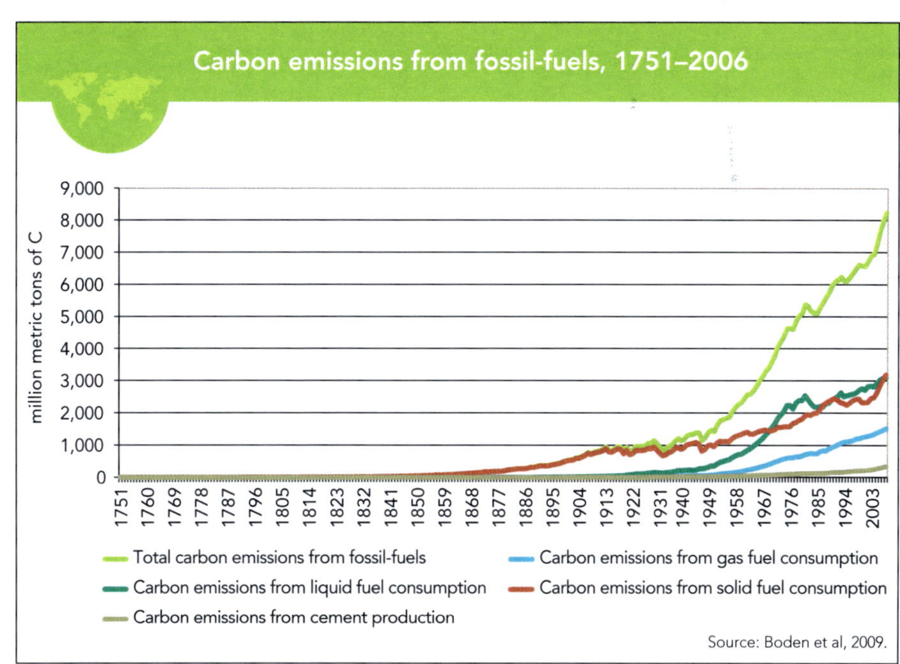

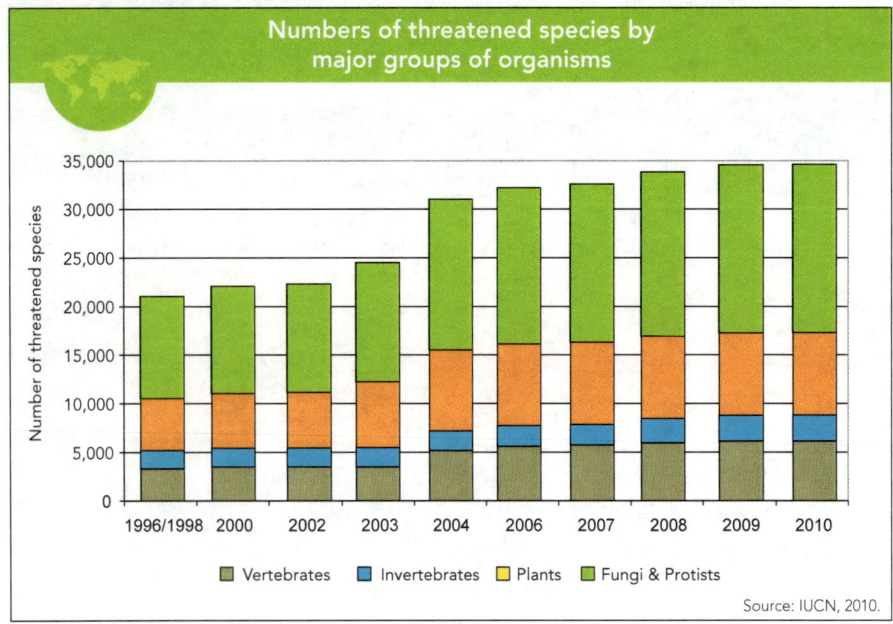

THE RATE OF BIODIVERSITY LOSS

The Millennium Ecosystem Assessment evaluated the ability of ecosystems to provide ecosystem services such as the provision of goods (e.g. food, water, fibre and fuel), the regulation of natural systems (e.g. climate, water and disease), cultural benefits (e.g. aesthetics, spiritual, recreation and education), and other supporting benefits (e.g. primary production and soil formation). The assessment concludes that humans have changed ecosystems in unprecedented ways over the last 50 years. Sixty percent of the world ecosystem services have been degraded, which is putting such strain on the natural functions of Earth that the ability of the planet's ecosystems to sustain future generations can no longer be taken for granted.[2]

The International Assessment on Agricultural Knowledge, Science and Technology for Development (IAASTD) finds that inappropriate fertilizer application has led to eutrophication and large dead zones in a number of coastal areas and some lakes, and inappropriate use of pesticides has led to groundwater pollution and loss of biodiversity. In addition, 1.9 billion hectares (and 2.6 billion people) are affected by significant levels of land degradation. The area of drylands has been growing steeply since the 1980s as a share of total land area. Very degraded soils are found especially in semi-arid areas, areas with high population pressure and in regions that are undergoing deforestation.

Biodiversity is highly correlated to the number and health of ecosystems. Vertebrates have been the most affected, with 10% of species threatened, followed by plant species with 3%.

INTERFERENCE WITH NITROGEN CYCLE

Nitrogen is needed to grow food but because of the inefficiencies of nitrogen uptake by plants and animals, only about 10 to 15 percent of reactive nitrogen is taken up. The rest is lost to the environment and injected into the atmosphere by combustion. This nitrogen pollutes water sources and the world's oceans, harming marine ecosystems, and contributes to global warming. Agricultural runoff and the burning of fossil fuels have boosted the supply of reactive nitrogen in the open oceans 50 percent above the normal range.[3]

Roughly four times more nitrogen fertilizer was applied in 2000 than in 1960, and applications have increased steadily since then. This has led to increased deposition and change in the N cycle in various ecosystems. Evidence suggests very high application rates contribute to soil degradation.[4]

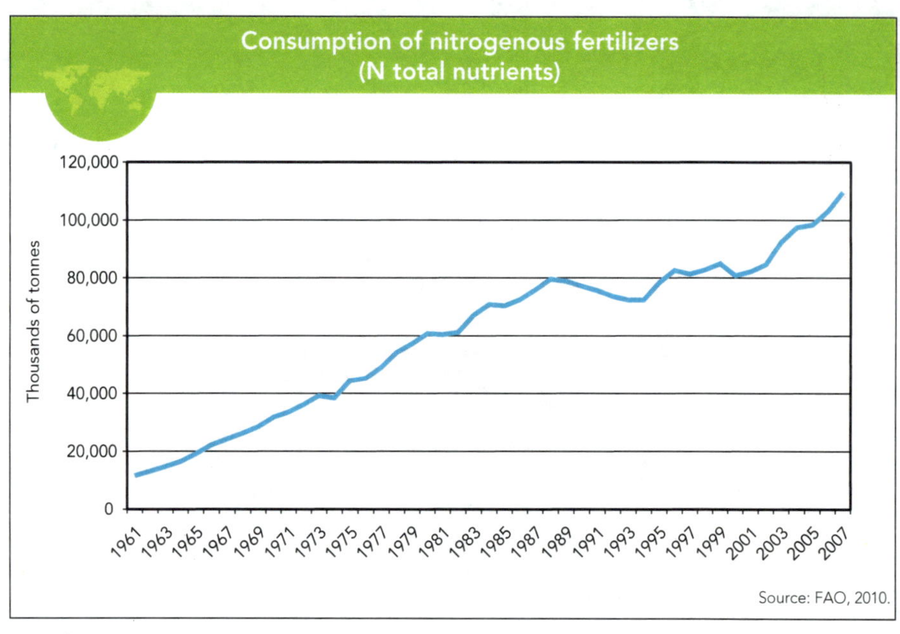

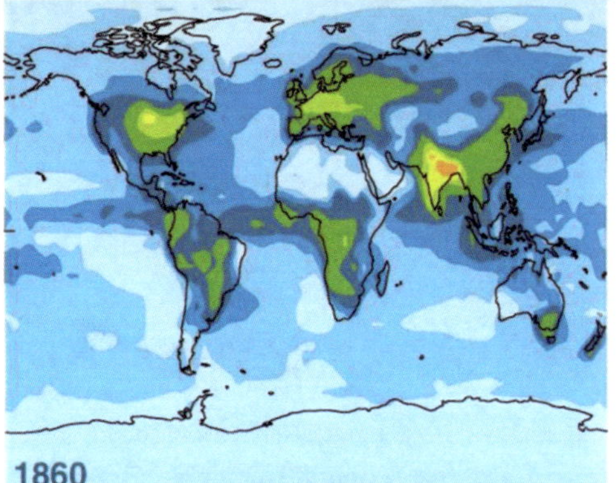

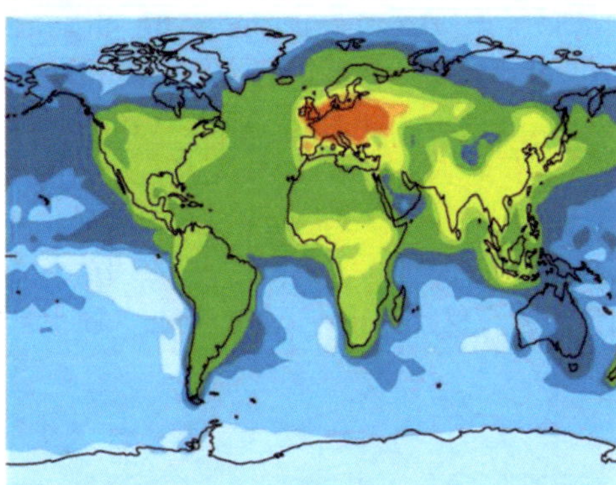

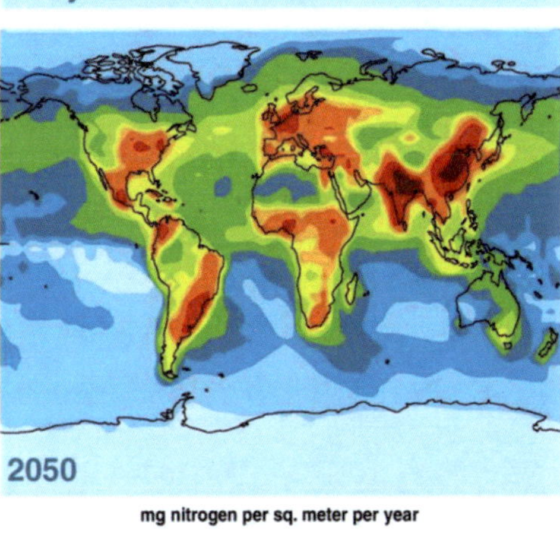

Source: UNEP/GRID-Arendal, 2005

ECOLOGICAL FOOTPRINT

Ecological Footprint analysis — which compares humanity's ecological impacts to the amount of biologically productive land and sea available to supply key ecosystem services (food supply, fibre, habitat, carbon storage, etc.) — finds that the global economy started exceeding the planet's biocapacity in the 1980s, and overconsumption of resources has increased since then.

The single largest demand humanity puts on the biosphere is its carbon footprint, which has increased tenfold since 1961. The Ecological Footprint exceeds the earth capacity to regenerate by 30%. Alternatively, 1.3 planets would be needed to stay within the planet's carrying capacity.[5] This is another, simplified way of picturing planetary boundaries and ecosystem thresholds.

Under a business-as-usual scenario, 2 planets would be required by 2030 to support the world's population. This assumes a continued unequal world with 15% of the population using 50% of the resources. World Wildlife Fund (WWF) estimates that three planets would be needed now if every citizen adopted the UK lifestyle, and five planets if they adopted the average North American lifestyle.

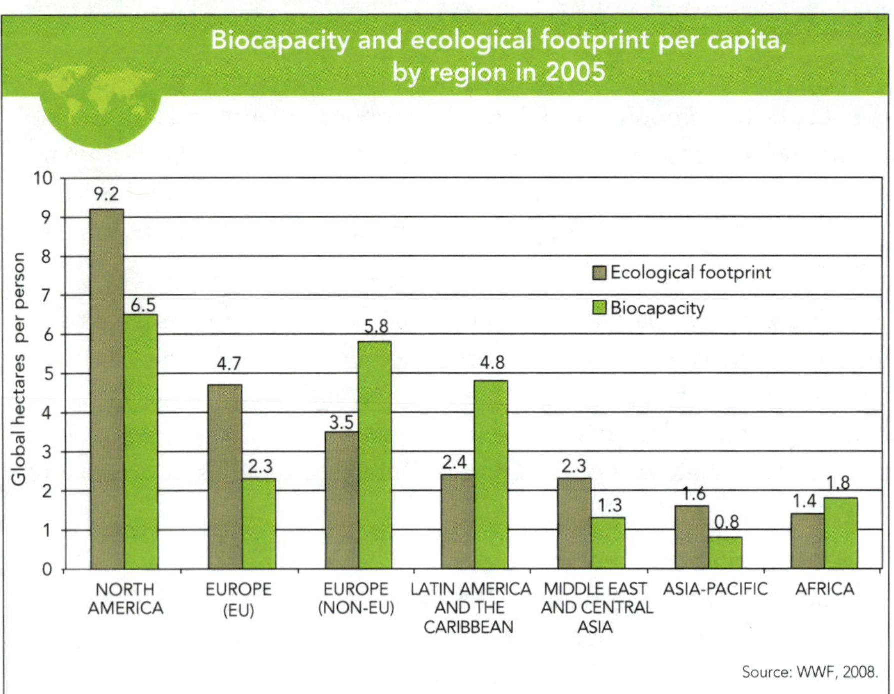

Regional differences are driven by differences in geography and climate, lifestyle, affluence, population and technological sophistication. At the regional and national level, a comparison of ecological footprints with biocapacity indicates whether countries and regions live within their biological carrying capacity (or "import" such capacity from the rest of the world).

The net balance of a country's footprint depends on its consumption compared to its biocapacity per capita.[5] Russia, Canada, the United States, Brazil, Australia, India, and Argentina have the largest biocapacity. Three of these have ecological footprints that exceed their biocapacity because of large population (China and India) or high consumption per capita (the US). Countries exceeding their biocapacity went from none in 1960 to 24 countries at present. North America, with the largest biocapacity per capita, still exceeds its biocapacity, while Africa with a relatively small biocapacity per capita and 902 million people has a biocapacity reserve.

> **As ecological reserves become increasingly rare, it will become critical ... to forge new relationships and move toward policies that protect natural assets while improving health and well-being. In this game, everyone can win. Every single person will benefit from early action.**
>
> — *Mathis Wackernagel,*
> *Executive Director of Global Footprint Network.*

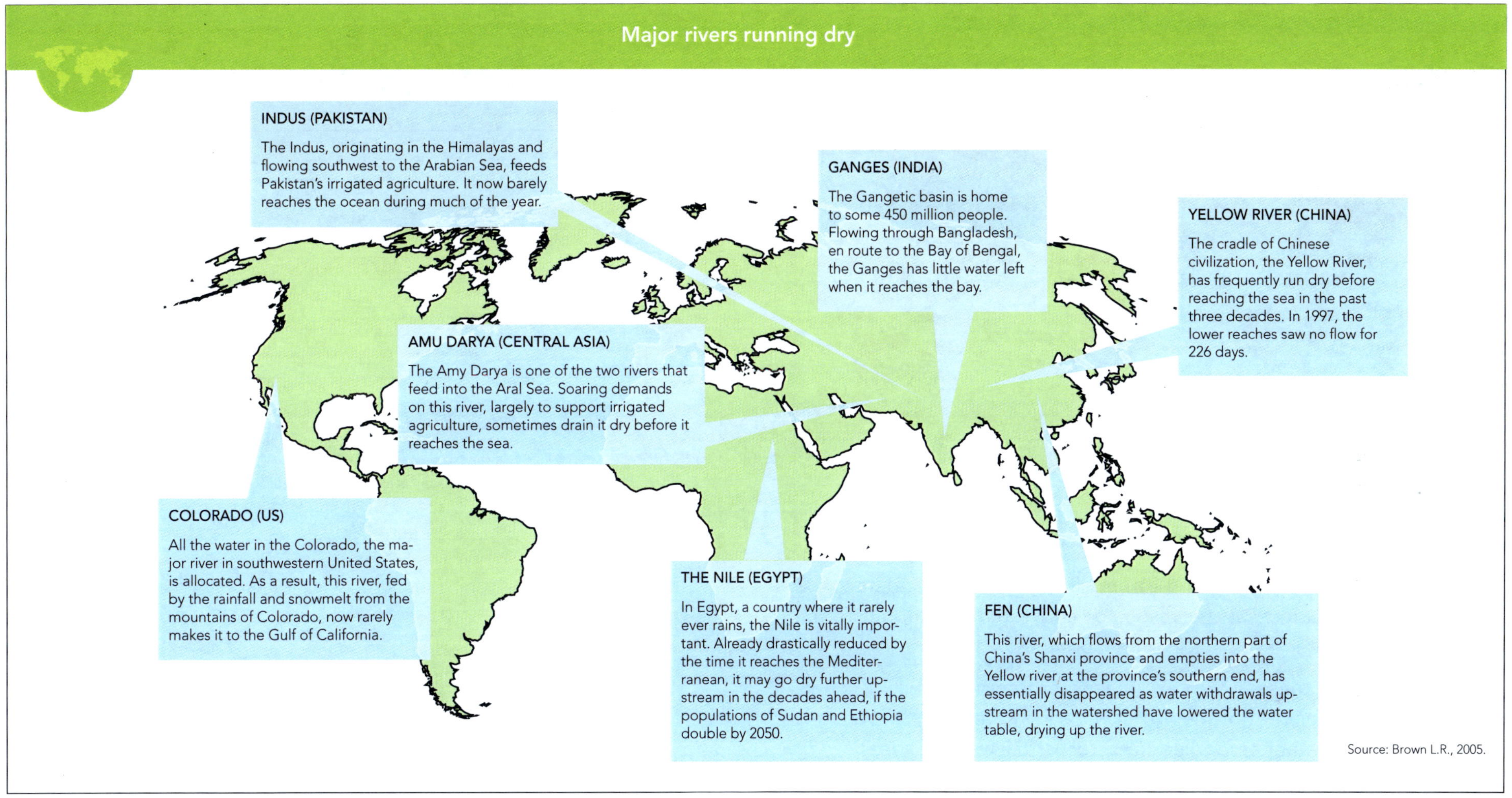

WATER FOOTPRINT

Local and regional imbalances between water availability and growing demand are a growing concern globally.

About 50 countries are already experiencing moderate to severe water stress all year round, while many others have water stresses during part of the year. Many lakes and rivers have dried out following extensive extraction and damming to irrigate agriculture.

Water-intensive agricultural products include meat, dairy products, sugar and cotton. Water use efficiency is often low, partly as a result of low water pricing or even subsidies, irrespective of scarcity. Lack of awareness of simple water saving measures among farmers and the use of water inefficient technologies also contribute. The water footprint of a country, an indicator introduced in 2002, measures the volume of freshwater used to produce the goods and services consumed by the inhabitants of a country, calculated over the product's entire global supply chain. It is composed

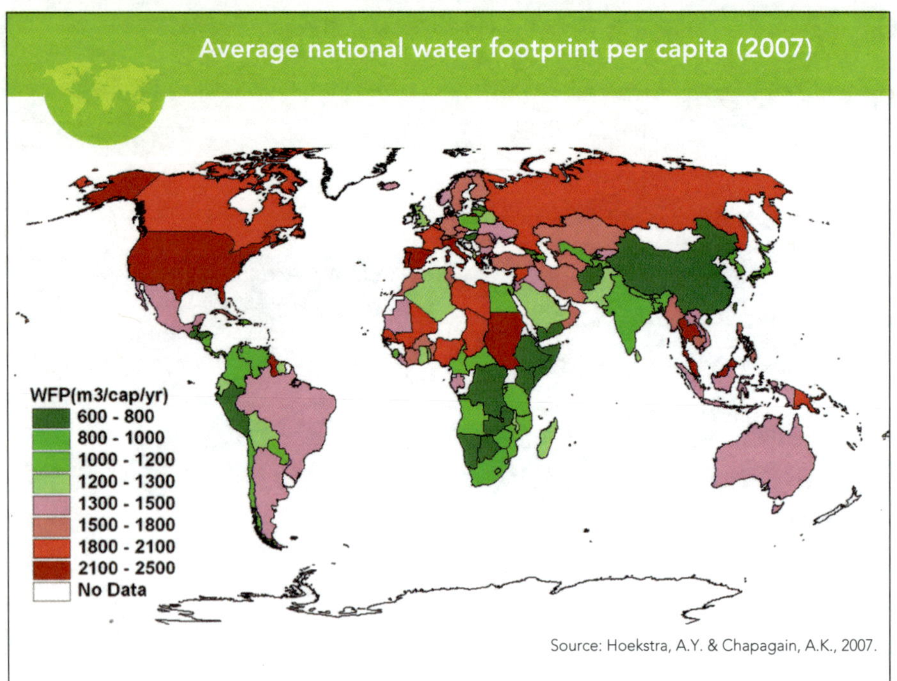

Average national water footprint per capita (2007)

Source: Hoekstra, A.Y. & Chapagain, A.K., 2007.

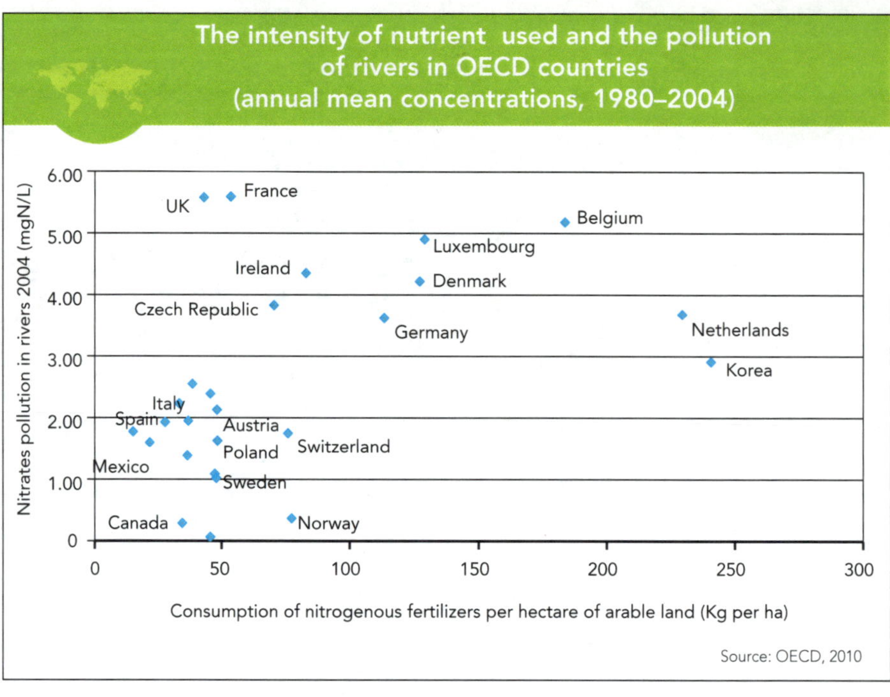

The intensity of nutrient used and the pollution of rivers in OECD countries (annual mean concentrations, 1980–2004)

Source: OECD, 2010

of the internal and external water footprint. Internal footprint refers to the appropriation of domestic water resources and external footprint to the appropriation of water resources in other countries.

Worldwide, 27 countries have an external water footprint which accounts for more than 50 per cent of their total water consumption, that is, they depend heavily on water-embodied trade (or 'virtual water' trade).

Major rivers and lakes, which serve as sources of drinking water, are increasingly polluted from both industrial and agricultural sources, including nitrogen. Generally, river pollution increases with nitrogen use intensity, though with considerable dispersion.

> **" You can't have sustainability if you are eating capital. Today we are consuming our natural capital. "**
>
> *— Pavan Sukhdev, study leader for the project on The Economics of Ecosystems and Biodiversity and the UNEP Green Economy Initiative*

III. DRIVERS OF CHANGING PRODUCTION AND CONSUMPTION PATTERNS

Though there are controversies around the way pressures on the planet's resources are measured, the message that consistently emerges is that the global economy is consuming resources at increasing and unsustainable rates. While substitution and new technologies can temporarily relieve resource pressures, the scale of use of finite resources continues to rise.

Delinking, or decoupling, refers to weakening or breaking the link between growth of economic activity and growth of consumption of materials, fossil fuels for energy and waste.

Delinking has occurred for some local environmental indicators, as rising incomes have been accompanied by improvements in access to clean drinking water and sanitation and some improvement in local and regional air quality. This has not been the case for other measures like waste generation, resource extraction and emissions of greenhouse gases. Even where delinking occurs it is in part the result of shifting resource extraction and production to other countries, including developing countries, as opposed to changes in patterns of consumption.

Growth in population, income and wealth over the next 40 years is expected to put increasing pressure on resources. Even if energy intensities of GDP continue to fall, the absolute levels of energy consumption are expected to continue rising and, without a major shift towards low-carbon energy, so too are CO_2 emissions.

Countries would appear to face a dilemma, as progress in human development (as measured by UNDP's HDI) is positively correlated with a country's ecological footprint. Few countries fall into the "sustainable development quadrant" of figure on the next page. The diagram illustrates well the notion of a dual convergence: in living standards (as those countries in the lower left quadrant would rapidly move to the lower right), and in environmental impacts (as those countries in the upper right quadrant would also move rapidly to the lower right).

The essential challenge facing humankind is to raise living standards and human development everywhere and for all while keeping within ecosystems' carrying capacities.

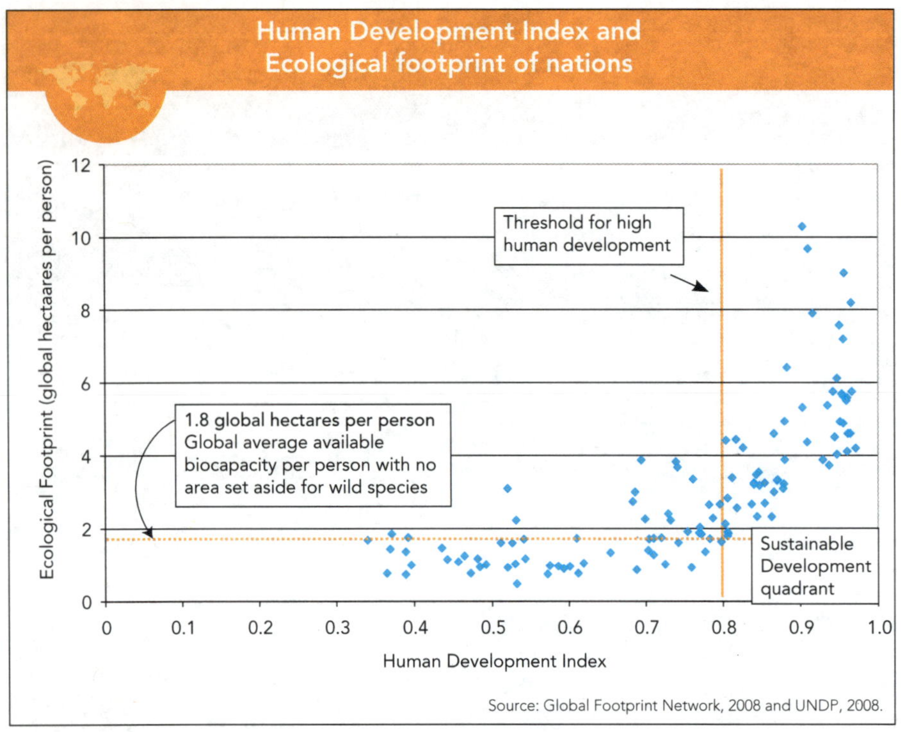

Source: Global Footprint Network, 2008 and UNDP, 2008.

AFFLUENCE

High-income countries have been characterized by a steady increase in the average per-person Ecological Footprint, from 3.5 global hectares in the early 1960s to roughly 6 global hectares at present.

As emerging economies become more affluent, the size of the global middle class is expected to increase, from fewer than half a million in 1960 to 4 billion in 2030. The largest number will live in China and India. Residential water and energy use, car ownership, personal travel, food — notably meat and dairy — consumption, and waste generation all increase with income.[6]

Moreover, consumption of some goods — e.g. consumer durables like automobiles — can increase very rapidly once middle class incomes pass a certain threshold. Car ownership plotted against per capita income shows a non-linear relationship. Ownership rates are usually minimal in the lowest income countries (clustered near the origin), but increase rapidly as per capita incomes rise above a threshold (around $10,000 per capita at purchasing power parity exchange rates).

> **"Without a fundamental shift in the way goods and resources are consumed, the world faces the prospect of multiple, interlocking global crises for the environment, prosperity and security. Sustainable consumption is a prerequisite for a more prosperous, safe and equitable global future."**
>
> *World Economic Forum*

Both energy consumption in general and oil consumption in particular rise with incomes. A number of the countries with the fastest GDP growth since 1980 also experienced rapid growth in energy use. This is not always the case, however. A few countries (for example Philippines, Bangladesh and Austria) had GDP growth per capita which was much faster than growth in per capita energy consumption.

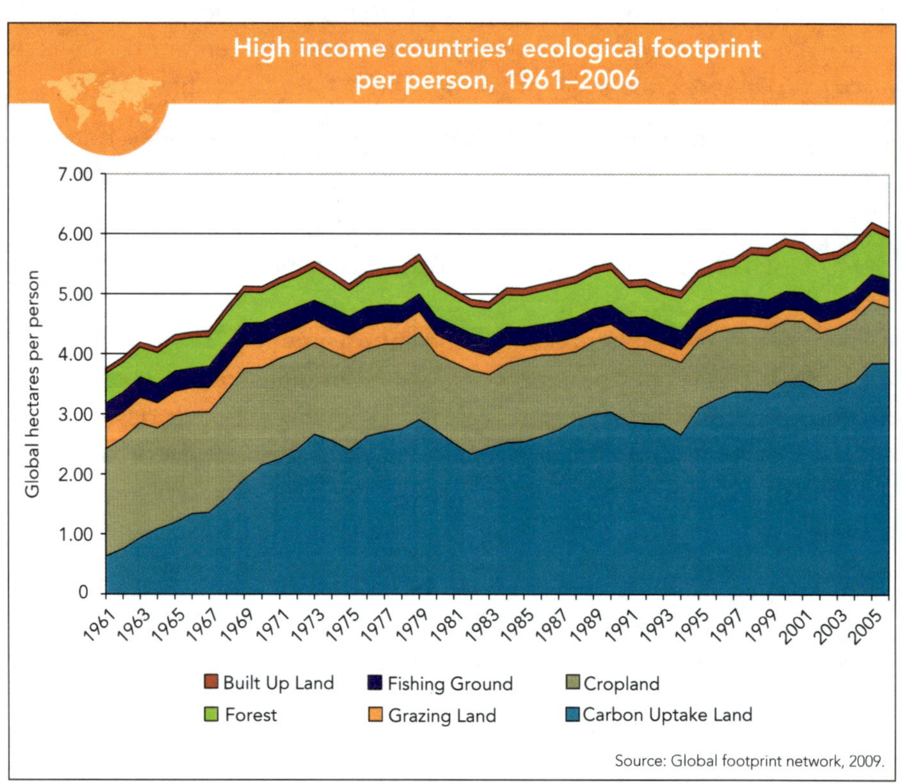

Source: Global footprint network, 2009.

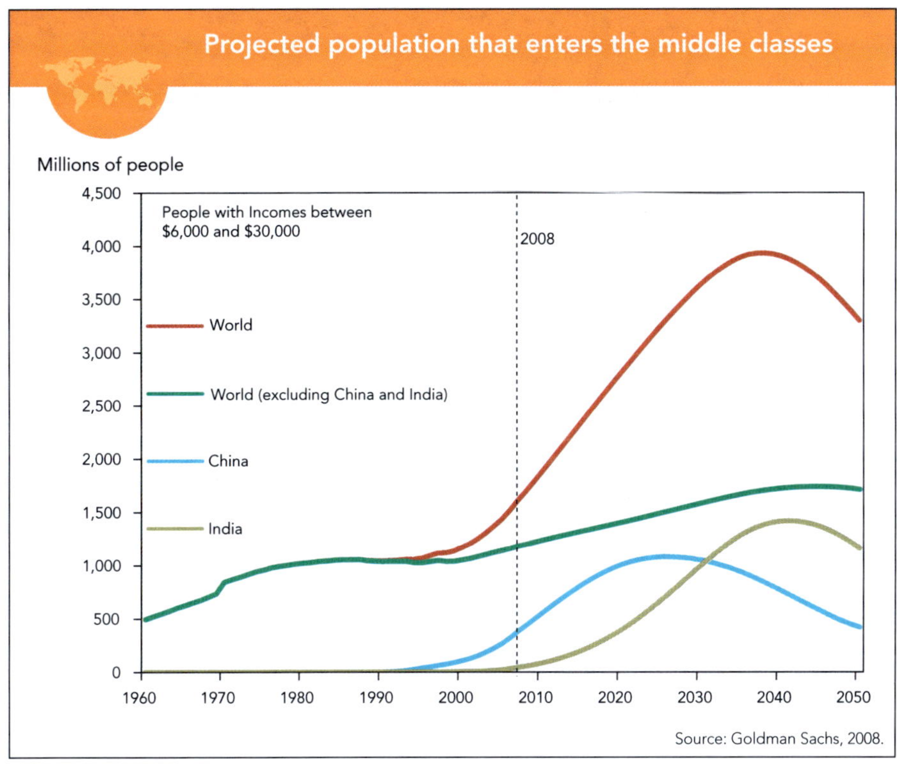

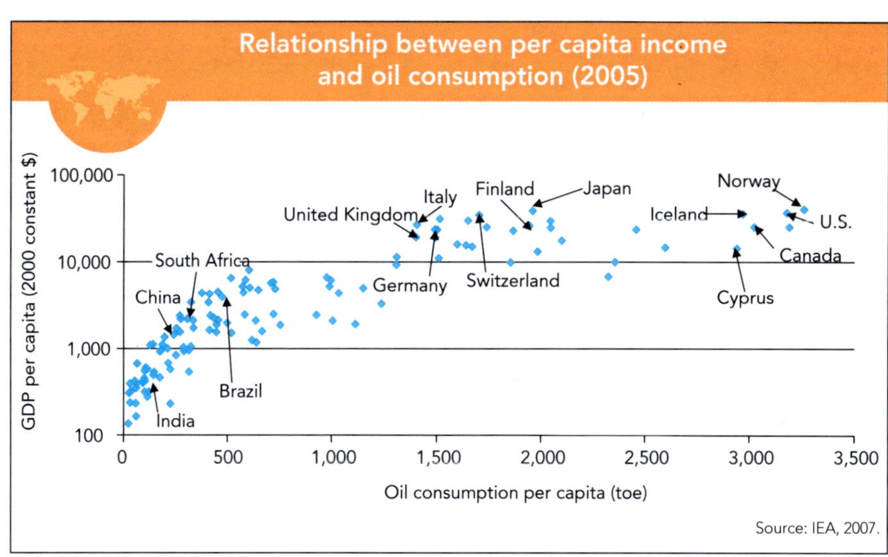

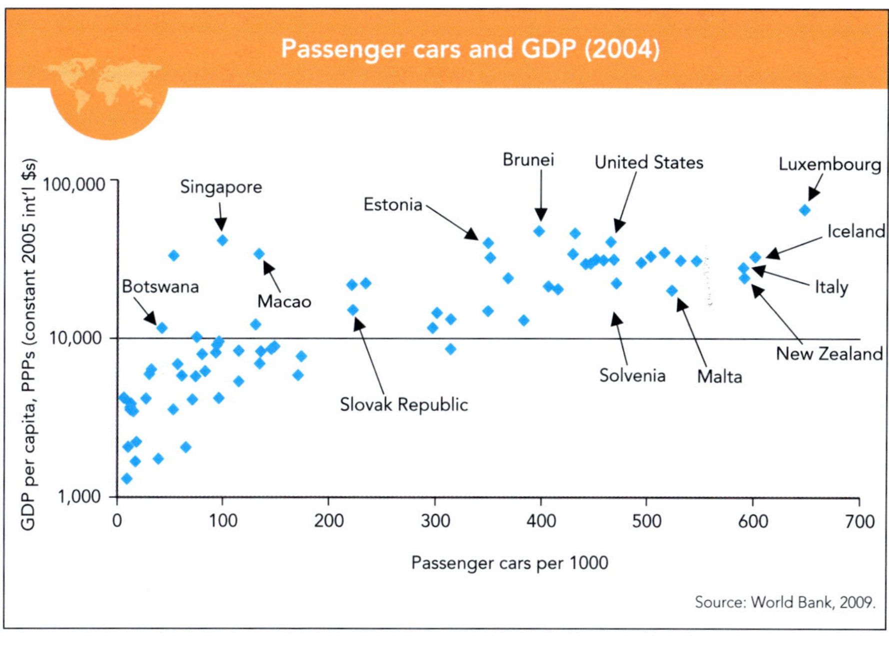

Also noteworthy is that for higher income levels there is a very wide range in car ownership per 1000 inhabitants, from the very high rates of Italy and New Zealand to the very low rate of Singapore. Size matters (to some degree) but so does government transport policy. Singapore, for example, invests heavily in public transport and uses a combination of regulation and economic incentives to limit private car ownership.

URBANIZATION

The planet's population is projected to rise above 9 billion in the second half of the century before leveling off. Between now and then, virtually all population growth will be in developing countries, with a very high proportion in cities.

As many of the countries where population is projected to rise have large numbers of people still living in poverty, levels of consumption will need

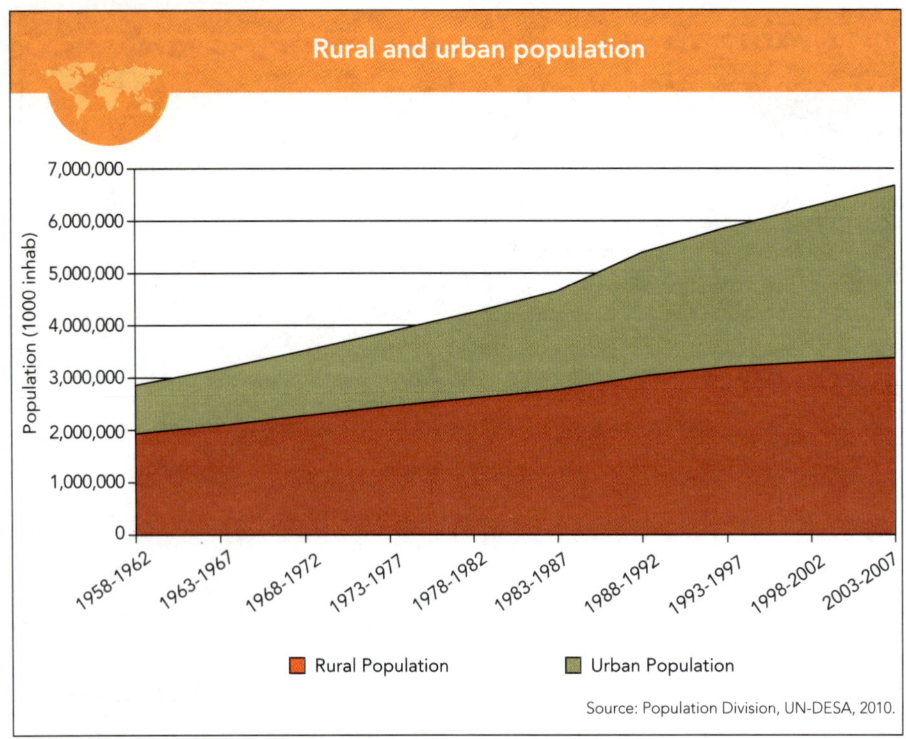

Source: Population Division, UN-DESA, 2010.

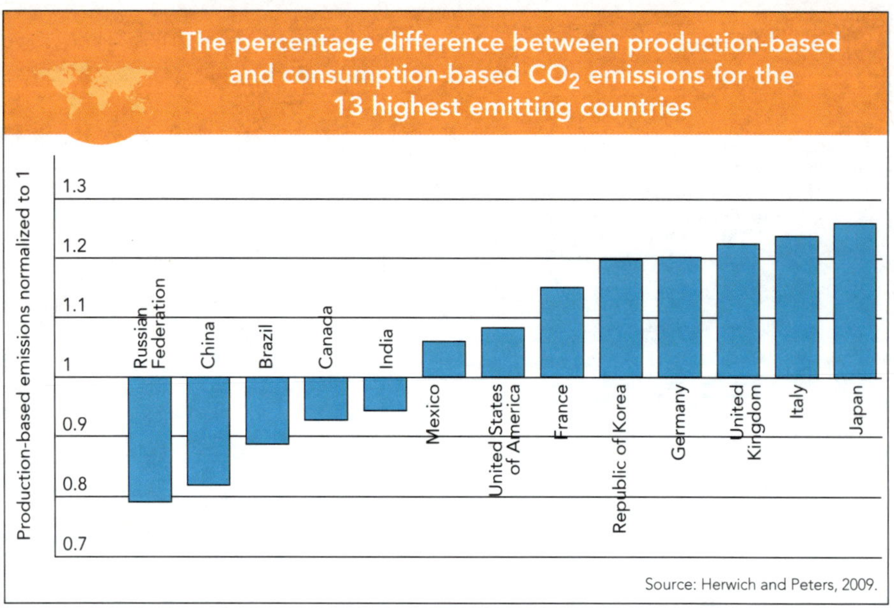

Source: Herwich and Peters, 2009.

to rise as well. As more join the ranks of the middle class, this will place additional pressure on planetary resources and ecosystems.

Hence the need for changing patterns of consumption and production, notably in developed countries, to relieve global resource pressures. Hence also the urgent need for diffusion across the globe of resource-efficient and energy-efficient technologies as well as renewable energy.

GLOBALIZATION

The globalization of production (and consumption) has brought opportunities to developing countries to raise their citizens out of poverty by participating in global production networks.

Yet, the growth in world trade and the global economy over the past several decades has not been matched by a growth in the capacity of nation-states and other actors to manage the consequences of growth for the global environment. Nor have the benefits of growth yet reached all.

Moreover, the (relative if not often absolute) decoupling of economic activity from resource use and pollution which has occurred in some developed countries has benefited from globalization, as resource- and energy-intensive activities are more and more concentrated in developing countries. On the other hand, the resource-intensity and pollution-intensity of consumption, considering entire product life cycles, is little changed.

This is illustrated by the difference between production-based emissions (all emissions produced within a nation's border) and consumption-based emissions (all emissions resulting from consumption within a nation) for the 13 highest emitting countries. Globalization has allowed production to be outsourced to rapidly developing countries, shifting the associated emissions to production activities in those countries, often for export back to developed countries.

IV. POLICY AND VOLUNTARY RESPONSES

With few exceptions, trends observed in earlier sections show resource use per capita rising with income albeit at different rates. Though the rate of increase may slow somewhat as countries become more developed and their markets for material-intensive products become saturated, in very few instances has there been a "bending of the curve" to the point where resource use, emissions and waste actually begin to decline while incomes continue to rise.

To make that happen requires more determined effort by all stakeholders. Increasingly, governments, companies, and various groups of civil society are working to find effective measures to delink resource use, waste, and harmful emissions from economic activity.

Governments have been using a number of measures: sustainable procurement; tighter efficiency standards for automobiles, appliances and new buildings; renewable energy portfolio standards and feed-in tariffs for electricity; various subsidies to promote greener products and services; and, in response to the economic crisis, green stimulus spending. Local authorities are both active and innovative in devising measures to promote sustainable cities and communities. In many cases, they are ahead of national governments.

The business sector is increasingly taking into account environmental and social issues, driven by a combination of government regulation, shareholder demands and consumer preferences and civil society pressure. Leading companies have set sustainability targets with timelines and regular reporting on progress, have signed on to voluntary pacts like the Global Compact and the Carbon Disclosure Project, and have engaged in a variety of partnerships with NGOs, academia and the public sector to bring their scientific, technical and managerial expertise and financial resources to bear on societal sustainability challenges.

> **States shall enact effective environmental legislation. Environmental standards, management objectives and priorities should reflect the environmental and developmental context to which they apply. Standards applied by some countries may be inappropriate and of unwarranted economic and social cost to other countries, in particular developing countries.**

— Principle 11, Rio Declaration on Environment and Development, 1992.

Civil society organizations have numerous local, regional, and national initiatives to raise consumer and citizen awareness, improve access to information, pioneer new market approaches (such as "fair trade"), and combine public pressure with constructive engagement with the private sector to change business practices.

GOVERNMENTS AND LOCAL AUTHORITIES

As governments are large consumers of certain products, their purchasing preferences can shape whole markets. Examples include: food, clothing, paper, electronic equipment, motor vehicles, electricity, and buildings.

Canada

A Policy on Green Procurement issued in April 2006 requires that environmental performance considerations be embedded into the procurement decision-making process in the same manner as price, performance, quality and availability. Guidelines, toolkits and training have been made available to facilitate this process. It is estimated that three quarters of government departments or agencies had green purchasing policies in place as of 2006/2007.

European Union

By early 2007, 9 out of 26 EU member-states had adopted national SPP or 'Green' action plans, 5 had drafted a national action plan but it had not yet been adopted, and 2 were in the process of preparing one. In Austria, Denmark, Finland, Germany, Netherlands, Sweden and the UK, 40 to 70% of all tenders published on Tenders Electronic Daily incorporated some environmental criteria, although in the remaining 18 countries, this figure was below 30%.

Japan

The 2000 Law on Promoting Green Purchasing makes it compulsory for government institutions to implement green procurement, while encouraging local authorities, private companies and individuals to make efforts for purchasing environmentally sound products and services. All state ministries, departments and agencies have to define procurement targets every fiscal year and make the results of green procurement efforts publicly available. 90% of central government agencies implement green procurement. Although by 2005 all sub-national governments had developed procurement policies, implementation has been slower.

United States

A 2007 Executive Order integrates and updates prior practices and requirements with the goal of increasing federal purchasing of energy efficient, recycled content, bio-based, and environmentally preferable products and services. Federal agencies must also ensure that: at least half of renewable energy comes from new renewable sources; water consumption is reduced by 2% annually through 2015; fleet total petroleum consumption is reduced by 2% annually, use of alternative fuels is increased by 10% a year, and plug-in hybrid (PIH) vehicles are used when available at reasonable costs.

Republic of Korea

The Act on the Promotion of the Purchase of Environment-Friendly Products, passed in 2005, requires public agencies at national and local levels to publish green procurement policies and implementation plans, carry out the latter, and report results. The Environment Ministry is asked to publish guidelines, designated items and evaluation criteria. Although green public procurement is still relatively small (roughly 6% of total public procurement in 2003), it has been growing very rapidly during the last years.

Mexico

The 2007-2012 National Development Plan created the scope for changes in procurement policy that allow for the incorporation of sustainability criteria. Recent changes in procurement law in Mexico include the requirement that all wood and furniture purchased by public agencies possess a certificate demonstrating its legal origin (since September 2007) and paper should have at least 50% recycled content.

Argentina

Argentina has developed an action plan to implement sustainable public procurement (SPP), and carried out research and training activities for procurement officials and policy-makers with the support of the Marrakech Task Force on SPP.

China

From January 2007, the central government and provincial governments are asked to give priority to environment-friendly products listed in a "green product inventory". The list, released in late 2006, includes products ranging from cars to construction materials that have been approved by the China Certification Committee for Environmental Labelling. Products are required to meet the environmental protection and energy saving standards set by the State Environmental Protection Administration in order to obtain the environmental label.

PromisE — Sustainable housing (Finland)

The Finnish Government has been working since the mid 1990s to make construction more ecologically sustainable. PromisE is an internet-based environmental classification system that has been developed to facilitate evaluations of the environmental properties of buildings in Finnish conditions. The system has two main versions: one for evaluating existing buildings and properties, and the other for use in the construction of new buildings. The PromisE system grades properties or individual buildings, and different versions can be applied to assess shops or commercial buildings as opposed to housing. Whole properties are assessed, including areas not built over. Environmental factors are divided into four main groups: health, use of natural resources, ecological impacts and environmental risk management. Each of these main areas includes a total of 35-40 indicators that can be measured numerically or otherwise evaluated. Both the private and public sector use PromisE.

Energy Efficient Public Buildings (France)

The goal of the French government is to reduce the energy consumption of existing buildings by at least 38 percent by 2020. To reach this goal France will start by 2012 the renovation of existing public buildings to reduce their energy consumption by 40 percent and their GHG emissions by 50 percent. As of 2010 the norm for new offices and public buildings will become 50 kWh/m/year.

Water for Everyone (Peru)

Water for Everyone program includes 270 projects in the water and sanitation sector. The upgrading of water and wastewater plants in many parts of the country will ensure the provision of clean water and reduce the time spent in fetching water. The program will deliver potable water to some 49,000 beneficiary families, and sewer service to some 57,000 families.

Green construction (South Korea)

In 2009 South Korea announced a green macroeconomic stimulus plan. At a cost of around U$36 billion over 2009 to 2012, the initiative aims to create 960,000 jobs, with 149,000 jobs expected to be created in 2009, mainly in construction. These low-carbon projects include developing railroads and mass transit, fuel efficient vehicles and clean fuels, energy conservation and environmentally friendly buildings. These measures alone will account for over 1.2 per cent of GDP, whereas the full stimulus plan involves investments of around 3 per cent of GDP.

Sustainable Public Transport and Sport (South Africa)

The South African government is building a new sustainable public transport system for the 2010 FIFA World Cup. The project is being implemented by UNDP, funded by GEF and executed by the South African Department of Transport, and aims to produce measurable environmental benefits including an estimated 423,000 tCO_2 reduction in direct GHG emissions over a ten-year lifespan, air quality improvement and reductions in ambient noise levels.

GRIHA (India)

GRIHA, Green Rating for Integrated Habitat Assessment, is a building 'design evaluation system' which aims to minimize the demand for renewable and non-renewable resources by focusing on reducing water and energy consumption, limiting waste generation through recycling, and reducing pollution. GRIHA emphasizes cost effectiveness and the integration of traditional heritage with scientific tools. GRIHA has 40 registered projects and recently the Government of India has announced that all government buildings must be at a minimum 3-star GRIHA compliant. In addition, the Energy Conservation Building Code (ECBC) has been made mandatory in eight States of India.

Chicago (The United States of America)

In 2007 Chicago set a tax on bottled water, becoming the first major U.S. city to impose such a surcharge. The Bottled Water Tax applies to the retail sale of bottled water in the City at a rate of $0.05 per bottle (i.e. all brands of non carbonated bottled water intended for human consumption). In addition to producing revenue that can be used to maintain the city's water infrastructure, the tax is designed to encourage citizens to shift their hydration habits from bottled to tap water, which is essentially the same thing you get when you buy most bottled water brands. The tax also helps in reducing the number of plastic containers that wind up in landfills (less than 20% of plastic water bottles in the United States of America are ever recycled) and reducing the greenhouse gas and other pollution created by trucking all that water to retail sites.

Mexico

In 2002 the Mexican government introduced reforms to reduce residential electricity subsidies. Households consuming between 280 and 500 kWh bimonthly face a gradual and differentiated reduction in their electricity rate subsidy, while households that consume more than 500 kWh will have the subsidy eliminated. The subsidy is retained for low-consumption households (less than 280 kWh), representing 75% of the population. The reduction in residential electricity subsidies is expected to generate revenues of 5 billion pesos. At the same time, a financial support programme will encourage the acquisition of more efficient refrigerators, air conditioners and insulation for consumers who live in hot regions.

Ireland

In March of 2002, Republic of Ireland became the first country to introduce a plastic bag tax, or PlasTax. Designed to rein in rampant consumption of 1.2 billion plastic shopping bags per year, the tax resulted in a 90% drop in consumption. To complete the win-win scenario, approximately $9.6 million was raised from the tax in the first year, which is earmarked for a green fund established to benefit the environment. Approximately 18,000,000 liters of oil have been saved due to reduced production of bags. Plastic bags are also taxed for example in Italy and Belgium, Taiwan and several Indian cities.

The Netherlands

The Netherlands, in 2001, through its Environmental Action Plan, increased energy prices for small-scale consumers by more than one-third by means of a tax levied on gas and electricity. Most of the tax revenues are redistributed to taxpayers through reductions in wage and income taxes, but a portion covers the cost of tax incentives for energy conservation measures. With the introduction of this tax, the price of household electricity has gone up by 15%.

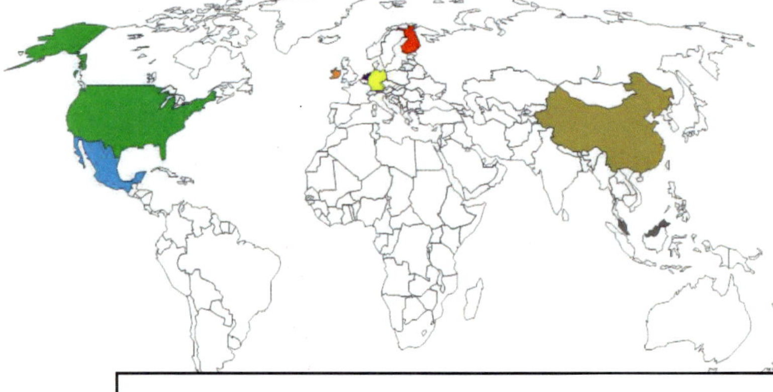

Malaysia

Malaysia was one of the first countries to use effluent charges, having introduced effluent fees, paired with licensing, to control pollution from the palm oil industry as early as 1977. Prior to the introduction of the regulation, crude palm oil was the single worst pollution source in the country. Daily discharge increased by more than 300% from 1965 to 1977. The regulation aims to reduce pollution in 42 rivers that were heavily polluted due to disposal of untreated effluents. A year after the imposition of the regulation, the pollution load fell more than half. Reduction in the pollution load decreased as well in the succeeding years. From 1977 to 1994, organic pollution load in the rivers decreased significantly by about 91%. As of 2006, of 1,064 water quality monitoring stations located within 146 river basins, almost 60% reported clean water while only 8% reported water that was categorized as very polluted.

Finland

Finland was the first country to implement a CO_2 tax in 1990, which today is among the highest in Europe. Without the impact of energy taxation, emissions would have been 7% higher than the 57 million tonnes recorded in 2000. The share of the carbon tax revenue is circa €500 million annually.

Germany

In 1999, Germany initiated its Ecological Tax Reform, gradually raising taxes on fossil fuels and electricity without increasing the overall tax burden. Electricity generated from renewable energy sources is exempt from the eco-tax, and electricity used by local public transport enjoys a 50% tax reduction. Some of the revenue is used to provide advice to homeowners on reducing energy consumption and for grants to schools for solar heating, photovoltaic panels and biomass energy systems.

China

China assesses levies on 29 pollutants in wastewater, 13 industrial waste gases, and various forms of industrial solid and radioactive waste. Regulated substances include SO_2, NOx, CO_2, hydrogen sulfide, dust, mercury, and lead. Plants pay a fee for emissions greater than the regulatory standard for each substance, but when more than one pollutant exceeds the standard, plants pay only for the single pollutant which will result in the largest fee. These effluent charges appear to have helped reduce both water and air pollution intensity during the period of rapid industrial growth in China since 1979. The effluent fees are also a major source of revenue for environmental projects. Of the fees collected, 80 percent are used for grants and low-interest loans for pollution control projects, and the remaining 20 percent refund local administration and monitoring activities.

EcoLogo (Canada)

Founded in 1988 by the Government of Canada and then transferred to a science-based environmental consultancy (TerraChoice) EcoLogoTM is North America's largest environmental standard and certification mark. EcoLogo provides customers with assurance that the products and services bearing the logo meet stringent standards of environmental leadership. There are thousands of EcoLogo Certified products covering a large variety of products and services ranging from carpets to car washed to motel categories. EcoLogo and GreenSeal are the two North American eco-labelling programs approved by the Global EcoLabelling Network as meeting internationally recognized ISO 14024 requirements.

Energy Star (United States)

© Energy Star is a joint voluntary program of the U.S. Environmental Protection Agency and the U.S. Department of Energy which was started in 1992 to reduce greenhouse gas emissions through energy efficiency. Energ Star is estimated to have saved enough energy in 2009 alone to avoid greenhouse gas emissions equivalent to 30 million cars —while saving nearly $17 billion in utility bills.To date, more than 30,000 commercial and industrial buildings have targeted energy efficiency improvements and more than 3,200 of these buildings have earned the Energy Star. Natural Resources Canada has also adopted the US Energy Star program for Canada.

Good Environmental Choice (Australia)

The Good Environmental Choice Label is the only environmental labelling program in Australia which indicates the environmental performance of a product from a whole-of-product-life perspective for consumer goods. The label is awarded to products that meet voluntary environmental performance standards which have been created and assessed in conformance to international environmental labelling standards.

Ecolabel (EU)

The European Ecolabel is a voluntary scheme, established in 1992 to encourage businesses to market products and services that are less damaging to the environment. Products and services awarded the Ecolabel carry the flower logo, allowing consumers — including public and private purchasers — to identify them easily. Today the EU Ecolabel covers a wide range of products and services, with further groups being continuously added. Product groups include cleaning products, appliances, paper products, textile and home and garden products, lubricants and services such as tourist accommodation.

Environmental Choice (New Zealand)

The New Zealand Ecolabeling Trust is a multiple specifications based environmental labelling programme, which operates to international standards and principles. It was initiated and endorsed by the New Zealand Government in 1990. Currently there are 14 product categories for products such as paints, office paper and stationery and thermal insulants amongst others. Environmental Choice New Zealand has over 1500 products that are registered as using the label.

Energy Label (Taipei, China)

To promote deployment of energy efficiency technologies and application of market incentive mechanisms, as well as to encourage manufacturers to invest in research and development of high energy efficiency products, the Bureau of Energy, Ministry of Economic Affairs, initiated the voluntary "Energy Label" program in 1992. The basis for determining the energy efficiency criteria of energy labeled products is to evaluate the energy performance of products on the market and select the middle to top performers on the efficiency distribution curve. The efficiency criteria are then periodically reviewed and revised to reflect the market conditions. These measures ensure creditability of energy label in denoting high energy efficiency products. The energy label is issued to individual product models only, not to the manufacturing system or corporation as a whole, and currently the label program covers 28 product categories and 4336 products with 258 brand names.

Eco-Label (South-Korea)

The Korea Eco-labeling Program is a voluntary certification program designed to encourage firms to provide consumers with a choice of environmentally sound products by displaying the designated logo (Eco-Label) and brief description. The purpose is to reduce consumption of energy and resources and to minimize generation of polluting substances in each production step. The Eco-labeling Program has been in place since 1992, and currently the scheme has 767 different categories of products such as batteries, wood products, beds and air-conditioners. In 2008 some 5,450 products of 1,179 companies had the label.

The GreenLabel (Singapore)

Singapore's GreenLabel programme was launched in May 1992 by the Ministry of the Environment as part of the country's national environmental management plan. It is a voluntary ISO Type I programme that is open to local and foreign companies conforming to the specified product criteria. As of January 2002, the programme applied to 29 product categories, covering a broad range of products, but excluding food, drinks and pharmaceuticals, as well as services and processes. More than 700 products currently have the GreenLabel, involving over 130 different manufacturers.

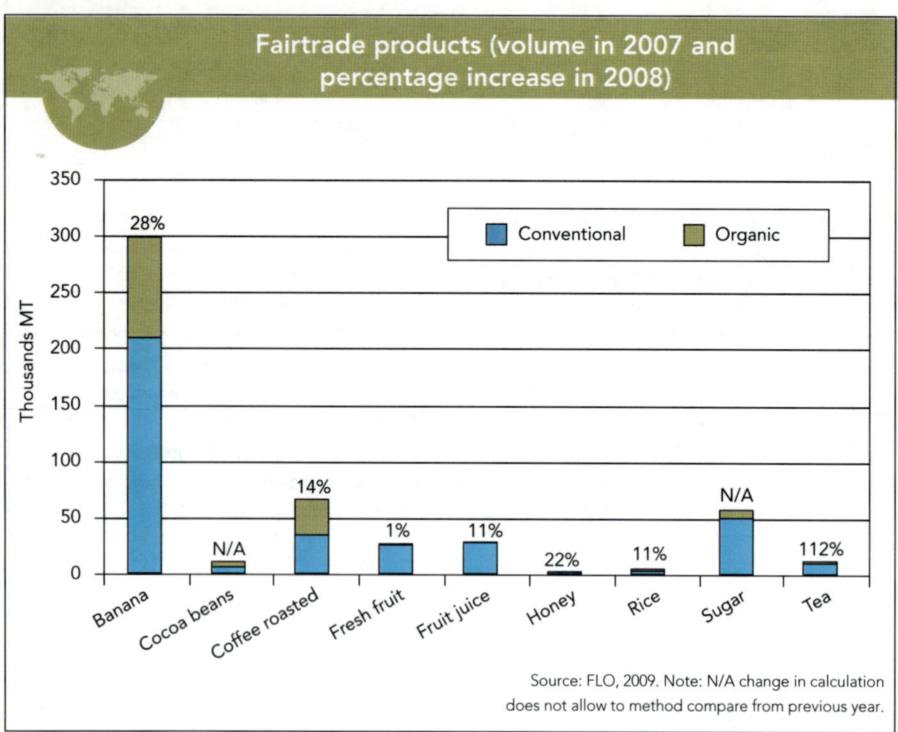

Source: FLO, 2009. Note: N/A change in calculation does not allow to method compare from previous year.

By the end of 2008, there were 746 certified Fairtrade producers world-wide, and over 2,700 companies are licensed to use the Fairtrade Mark on products. The estimated retail value of Fairtrade products rose 22% to almost € 2.9 billion while fairtrade sales grew by 50% or more in seven countries, despite the recession, and no markets fell back. Tea saw the largest 2008 growth rate (112% from 2007), albeit from a very small base. In addition to products illustrated in the figure, over 27 million items made of Fairtrade certified cotton were sold, almost double the sales of 2007. Sales of bananas grew by 28% to almost 300,000 metric tons and those of honey by 22%. Almost nine million litres of Fairtrade wine were consumed — an increase of 57%. Standards have now been established for olives and olive oil, soybean, haricot beans, chickpeas and lentils. Several revised standards allow more farmers of mangoes, bananas, pineapple and vanilla to enter the market as well. These growth rates are expected to continue. The first ever global consumer survey on Fairtrade was conducted in 2008 and found that half of the public are now familiar with the Fairtrade Mark. The survey found that 'active ethical consumers' make up more than half the population (55%) in the countries surveyed.[7]

> **The needs of small farmers, whether they grow coffee [in the South] or produce [in the North], may be quite similar. Both groups need better access to and more control over the market. That can only happen if consumers use their market power to vote for fair prices to the grower, better access to financing for small farmers, and more environmentally sustainable production.**

> — *Rink Dickinson, Co-Director, Equal Exchange*

Energy labels (EU)

According to several different EU Directives most domestic appliances, light bulb packaging and cars must have an EU Energy Label clearly on display when it is offered for sale or for rent. The Energy Rating label enables consumers to compare the energy efficiency of appliances. It is also an incentive for manufacturers to improve the energy performance of their products. The energy efficiency of the appliance is rated in terms of a set of energy efficiency classes from A to G on the label, A being the most energy efficient, G the least efficient. Recently A+ and A++ grades were introduced for refrigeration products.

Regulating greenhouse gas emissions from cars (United States of America)

In 2010 the White House finalized rules on the first U.S. greenhouse gas emission standard for automobiles, which would raise average fuel economy 42 percent by 2016 in a bid to slash oil imports and fight climate change. The higher mileage requirements will reduce U.S. greenhouse gas emissions by 900 million metric tons and save 1.8 billion barrels of oil over the life of vehicles built during the 2012-2016 model years, according to the Environmental Protection Agency. The vehicle emissions standards will be phased in starting with the 2012 model year, raising fuel economy to an average 35.5 miles per gallon by the time the 2016 models are ready compared with the current 25 pg.

Phosphate reductions in laundry detergents (Sweden)

Phosphorus emissions from sources such as detergents and cleaning agents contribute to eutrophication in lakes and seas. In 2008 the Government of Sweden introduced a ban on retail sales of laundry detergents containing phosphates. The Government intends to introduce a ban on phosphates in dishwasher detergents for private use from 1 July 2011. The ban means that it will not be permitted to manufacture or market dishwasher detergents with a phosphorus content of more than 0.5 per cent by weight.

Energy Performance Certificate (England and Wales)

The Energy Performance Certificate (EPC) was first introduced for the sale of existing homes, as part of the Home Information Pack. Since 1 October 2008, when buildings are built, sold or rented, an EPC has been required. From April 2008 this was extended to newly built homes and large commercial properties. The certificate provides energy efficiency A-G ratings and recommendations for improvement. The ratings — similar to those found on products such as fridges — are standard so the energy efficiency of one building can easily be compared with another building of a similar type.

Energy Label (China)

China is now one of the world's largest producers and consumers of household appliances, lighting, and other residential and commercial equipment. In 2005 China started a mandatory energy information label, the Energy Label. It includes five categories of efficiency, from 100% (meeting the minimum standard) to 55% of the minimum standard. The label initially covered two products and in 2007 was extended to cover four products including air conditioners, household refrigerators, clothes washers, and unitary air conditioners.

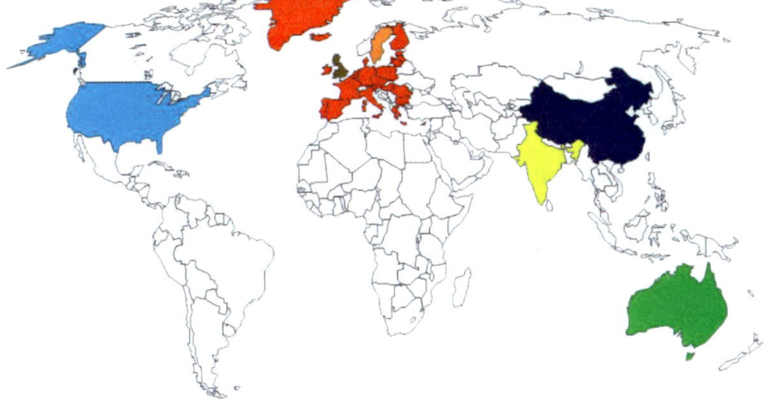

Eco-Labeling (India)

To increase consumer awareness, the Government of India launched the eco-labeling scheme known as 'Ecomark' in 1991 for easy identification of environment-friendly products. Any product which is made, used or disposed of in a way that significantly reduces the harm it would otherwise cause the environment could be considered as Environment-Friendly Product. The criteria follow a cradle-to-grave approach, i.e. from raw material extraction, to manufacturing, and to disposal. The 'Ecomark' label is awarded to consumer goods which meet the specified environmental criteria and the quality requirements of Indian Standards. As a continuation to Ecomark, starting in January 2010, it will become mandatory for certain products to carry eco-labeling in India. Firstly four products — refrigerators, air conditioners, distribution transforms and florescent lamps — will be covered. By summer 2010 three more product lines (color TVs, LPG stoves and electric motors) will need to carry the mandatory eco labeling.

Energy efficiency light bulbs (Australia)

In February 2007 Australia announced a plan to establish energy efficiency standards for light bulbs that would ban incandescent bulbs by 2010, with both regulatory and persuasive measures used to induce a shift to compact fluorescent bulbs (CFLs). According to the Federal Government, up to 95 per cent of the energy each standard light bulb uses is wasted, while compact fluorescents use only 20 per cent as much electricity to produce the same amount of light. It is estimated that household lighting costs will be reduced by up to 66% and that CO_2 emissions will be reduced by 800,000 tonnes per year for the 2008-2012 period. Cuba and Venezuela also have national programmes to replace incandescent bulbs with compact fluorescents. Similar measures were taken in the European Union in 2009.

United States of America (Portland, Oregon)

Rated as the greenest city in America, half of Portland's power comes from renewable sources, a quarter of the workforce commutes by bike, carpool or public transportation, and the city has 35 buildings certified by the U.S. Green Building Council. Portland aims to be a "20 Minute City" where residents spend 20 minutes or less traveling from home to work, shop or play.

United Kingdom (Beddington Zero Energy Development)

Beddington Zero Energy Development is the UK's largest mixed use sustainable community of 100 households. It was completed and occupied in 2002. 86% of BedZED residents buy organic food and 39% grow some of their own food. The residents only use 72 litres of mains water per day, topped up by 15 litres of recycled or rainwater.

China (Panyu Jinshan, Guangzhou)

This will be a community of 8,000 homes along with a community centre and some retail units. The aim is to achieve 65% reductions in energy demand and 50% reduction in water demand. The plans for Panyu Jinshan include developing a 'cultural street' and space for local Cantonese Opera, and solar hot water panels on all the possible roof areas in the development.

Green Building in US and the world

The floor area registered and certified to the LEED green building rating system in 2009 is estimated to grow by over 40 percent compared to last year's totals, for a cumulative total of over 7 billion square feet worldwide since the standard was launched in 2000. Non-U.S. green buildings reached nearly 800 million square feet of registered projects in 2009, representing more than a fourth of all project square footage. Non-U.S. LEED projects could show a 30% increase in registration this year, thanks in large part to green building booms in China, India, and the Middle East. Green building is also growing quickly in Europe, notably Germany and Italy.

Barangaroo (Australia)

Barangaroo is a 22 ha site in the heart of Sydney whose construction towards a sustainable community is due to start in December 2010, with 350,000m2 of commercial space and 500 residential units planned for development. The aim is to reach a 75% reduction in energy demand compared to business as usual, a 20% reduction in embodied energy, 87% diversion from landfill of operational waste, with a 100% reduction in greenhouse gases and a 4% car use modal split

United States of America (Sonoma Mountain Village, California)

Full construction started on site in 2009 with first residents moving in during 2010. This 200 acre (81 ha) site will accommodate 1,892 homes, and 825,000 square feet (76,645 m^2) of office, retail and commercial space. An 83% reduction in total household direct carbon emissions is targeted.

Portugal (Mata de Sesimbra)

An integrated sustainable building, tourism, nature conservation and reforestation programme. The 5,300 hectare site will contain a 4,800 hectare nature reserve and native pine, cork and oak forest restoration project, alongside a 500 hectare tourism development comprising around 5,000 units. The development will go on to meet 'zero waste' targets, while 50 per cent of food will be sourced from local sources. The site will use 100% renewable energy and the transport network is designed virtually to eliminate private cars.

United Arab Emirates (Masdar city)

This will be the world's first zero-carbon, zero-waste, car-free city. The city's electricity and cooling will be provided by renewable energy generated on site. Water consumption will be reduced by over 50% compared to the Abu Dhabi baseline. Masdar City will cover 6 km^2 and house 50,000 people and 1,500 businesses. An expected 40,000 workers will commute to the city daily. The first phase is scheduled to be complete and habitable in 2009, with full completion due around 2016.

BUSINESSES

Corporate environmental and social responsibility has become a higher profile management concern in recent years in many countries. Membership in a number of global initiatives reflects this, including the Global Compact, the Global Reporting Initiative, the Carbon Disclosure Project and ISO14000 certification of corporate environmental management systems as well as the development of ISO26000.

All these are voluntary initiatives. The first stresses adherence to common principles of corporate conduct and regular reporting, the next two emphasize information disclosure, while the last uses international certification to convey in summary form information about environmental management.

The number of Global Compact signatories and the number of GRI reporters have both increased sharply since the middle of the past decade. As of 2008, GC signatories exceeded 6,000 and there were 5,300 active business participants from more than 135 countries.

The business case for sustainability, World Economic Forum, January 2009

The International Standards Organization (ISO) provides a widely recognized set of standards for products and processes, including environmental management processes of enterprises. ISO 14001 certification signals potential customers or partners that a company meets certain standards with respect to internal controls on materials use, energy use, pollution and waste, and that it is committed to continuous improvement.

The number of enterprises certified to ISO 14001 has been rising steadily, from under 40,000 in 2001 to almost 160,000 in 2007. It is a particularly well utilized practice for exporters to obtain ISO 14001 certification as a means of informing consumers in their export markets of their environmental performance. This is one reason for the large weight of China and Japan in the total number of certificates issued.

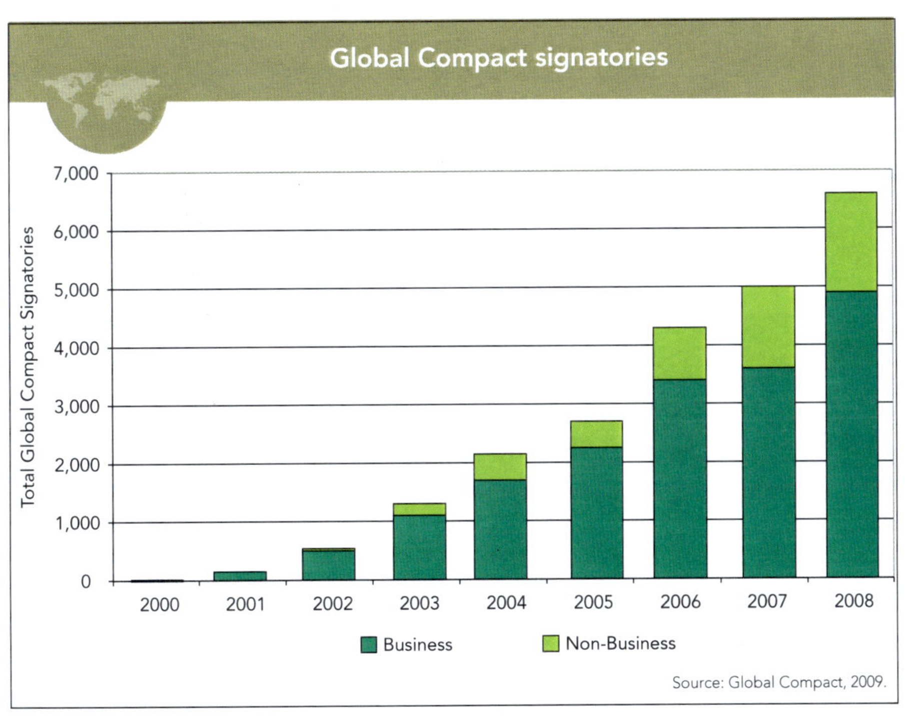

Source: Global Compact, 2009.

Source: ISO, 2008.

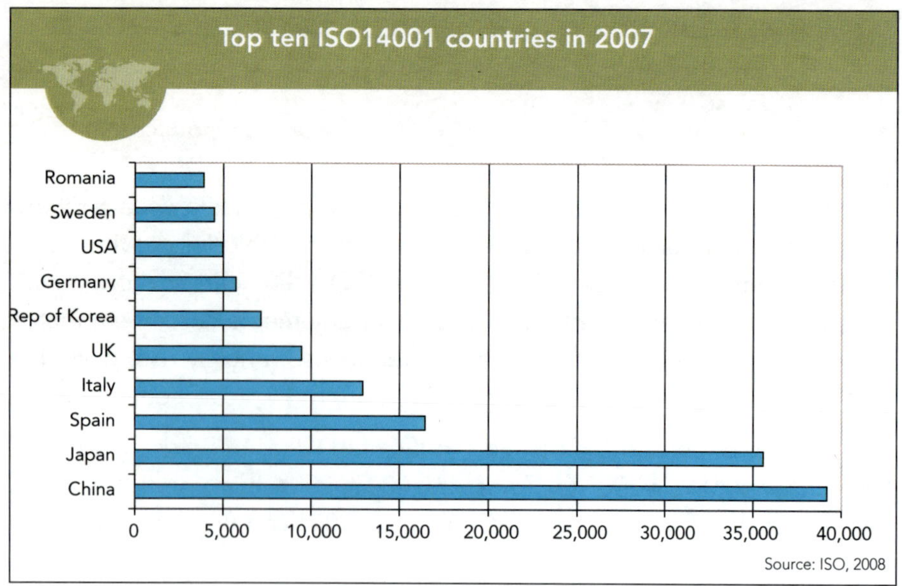

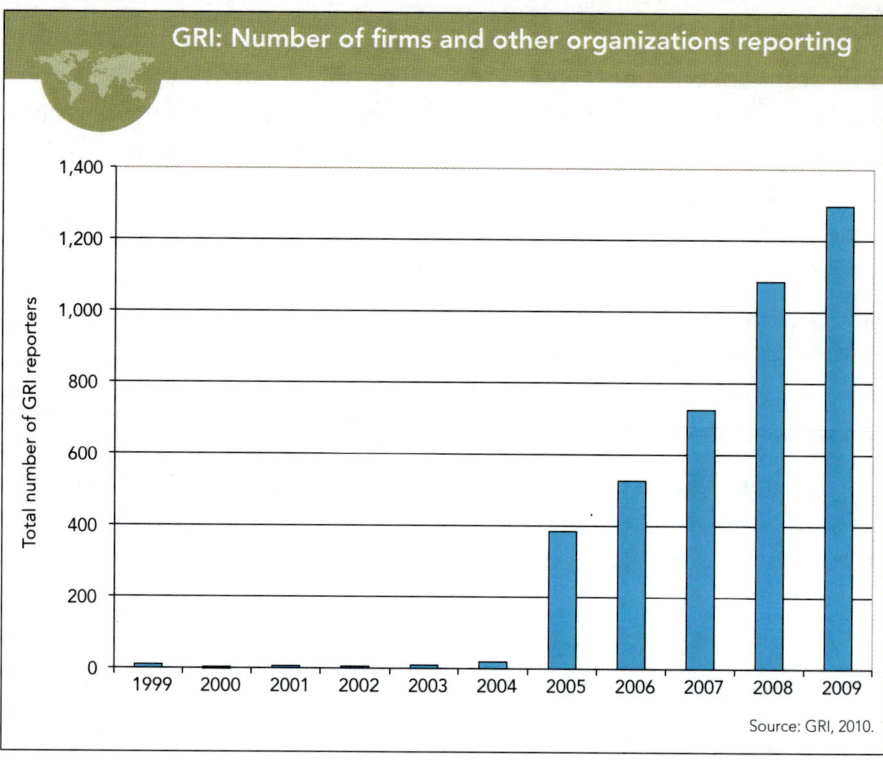

As of 2009, the Global Reporting Initiative (GRI) counted over 1,200 organisations worldwide, many private corporations, that issued sustainability reports based on its GRI G3 Guidelines — an increase of 46% over 2007.

The Global Reporting Initiative (GRI) is a network-based organization that has development the world's most widely used sustainability reporting/disclosure framework through a consensus-seeking process with participants drawn globally from business, civil society, labor, and professional institutions. This framework sets out the principles and indicators that organizations can use to measure and report their economic, environmental, and social performance. The aim of the GRI is that disclosure of these performance become as commonplace and comparable as financial reporting, and as important to organizational success.[8]

> **Business is the force of change. Business is essential to solving the climate crisis, because this is what business is best at: innovating, changing, addressing risks, searching for opportunities. There is no more vital task.**
>
> *Richard Branson, Founder, Virgin*
> *http://www.mjcsustainability.com/*

Electrolux (Sweden)

The biggest environmental impacts from appliances occur during the use phase. Developing and selling energy and water efficient appliances is therefore the most important contribution Electrolux can make to meet the climate challenge. Electrolux's 2009 target to reduce energy use in operations by 15% compared to 2005 was exceeded, and it is now aiming at more stringent target of reducing energy use by close to 30% by 2012 compared with 2005.

Philips digital Dictaphone (The Netherlands)

A good example of product eco-design is Philips' new Digital Pocket Memo® 9600/9620. Its life cycle assessment was carried out in accordance with ISO 14040, and significant energy savings were realized due to interaction of state-of-the-art components and an improved firmware and energy management. The new model allows up to 17 hours of dictation without recharging the batteries. The possibility to charge the rechargeable batteries by connecting the device to a USB helps to reduce Standby Energy consumption. The LCA shows significant reduction in Global Warming Potential (GWP): depending on the mode of operation, up to 86.1% reduction is possible in comparison to the previous model.

Voluntary Green Standards (US)

The Electric Utility Industry Sustainable Supply Chain Alliance has developed a set of voluntary standards which define best practices to help non-fuel suppliers assess the environmental performance of their companies and utilities, and the environmental performance of their supply chain operations. The Alliance is also developing voluntary environmental standards for products and services purchased by electric utilities, starting with wood poles, transformers, and wire and cable.

AkzoNobel (The Netherlands)

AkzoNobel is the largest global paints and coatings company. AkzoNobel is now partnering with maritime classification society Lloyd's Register to introduce China's largest shipyards to the Performance Standard for Protective Coatings (PSPC), offering shipyards step-by-step advice on how to go about meeting the requirements of the new standard. They are advising the shipping industry on, for example, antifouling coatings which make shipping more efficient by preventing organisms such as barnacles and weed from building up on the underwater hull, slowing the ship and decreasing fuel efficiency. It is estimated that the use of antifouling coatings saves the shipping industry around US$30 billion and reduces CO_2 and SO_2 emission levels.

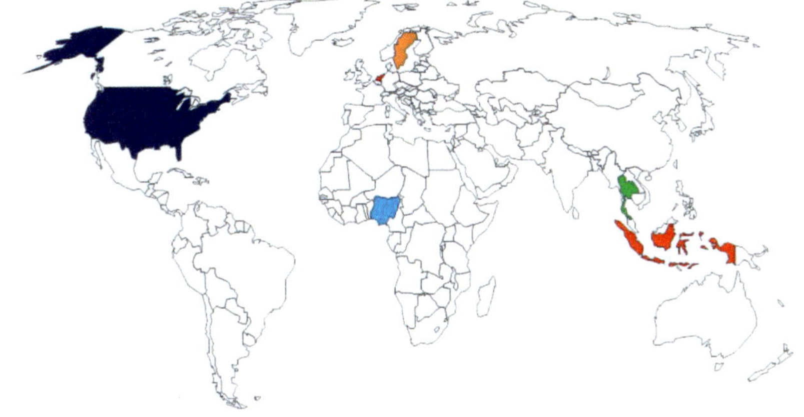

Diageo (Nigeria)

Two decades ago, all the grain for Diageo's breweries in Africa was imported. The imports required precious foreign currency and represented a lost business opportunity for local farmers. Diageo joined a project to develop the cultivation of a beer-friendly variety of sorghum in Nigeria. The project identified a usable sorghum cultivar and trained farmers to grow the crop. Sorghum farmers reported a 35-50% increase in yield from their land. Today, Diageo breweries in Nigeria source 95% of their grain from local farms, sustaining around 27,000 jobs. Diageo is a signatory to the UNDP's Business Call to Action (BCtA) which seeks to accelerate progress toward the achievement of the Millenium Development Goals by encouraging private sector investment in base of the pyramid markets.

Sustainable Palm Oil Roundtable (Indonesia)

The Sustainable Palm Oil Roundtable, a non-for-profit organization, develops standards for sourcing sustainable palm oil in what is both a highly important industry for developing economies and, currently, one that is highly destructive of tropical forests. Vegetable oil production worldwide totals 95 million tonnes per year, of which over 28 million tonnes is palm oil, the world's second largest oil crop after soy oil.

The Green Label Scheme (Thailand)

The Thai Green Label Scheme was initiated by the Thailand Business Council for Sustainable Development and formally launched in August 1994 by the Thailand Environment Institute and the Ministry of Industry. The Green Label certificate is awarded to products that are shown to have minimum detrimental impact on the environment in comparison with other products serving the same function. More than 137 products in 18 categories have received the Green Label certificate.

■ UNIDO/UNEP Cleaner Production Centers (Global)

UNIDO in cooperation with UNEP started, in 1994, to set up National Cleaner Production Centers and Programs. Since then, 43 centers and programs have been established in developing and transition countries, with others in the planning stage. The centers and programs train enterprise leaders in cleaner production helping them to adopt and adapt practices to local conditions. The programs also aim to foster dialogue between industry and government and enhance investments for transfer and development of environmentally sound technologies to bridge the gap between competitive industrial production and environmental concerns. With the program, costly end-of-pipe pollution control systems are gradually replaced with a strategy that reduces and avoids pollution and waste throughout the entire production cycle, from efficient use of raw materials, energy and water to the final product. Successful programs have been implemented in, for example, Bulgaria, Cambodia, Costa Rica, Cuba, India, and Nicaragua.

■ Responsible Environmental Marketing Communications (Global)

To help marketers and advertisers avoid the mistakes of vague, non-specific or misleading environmental claims, the International Chamber of Commerce has produced a global Framework for Responsible Environmental Marketing Communications. The framework includes a practical checklist aimed at the creators of marketing communications campaigns, as well as a chart that provides an easy reference to relevant provisions of the global advertising code and offers more detailed interpretations on current issues related to environmental marketing.

■ Education on sustainable small-scale farming (The Netherlands)

Learning AgriCultures is a learning resource particularly useful for educators seeking support material for explaining about sustainable agriculture in their courses, at a university or college level, in special NGO training courses or elsewhere. The series aims to stimulate learning about sustainability issues for small-scale farmers through a systems thinking perspective.

■ Education for sustainable consumption (Global)

Considering the role of education as a key instrument to achieve sustainable development, Italy set up an international task force on education for sustainable consumption. Under the Marrakech Process it has produced a set of recommendations and guidelines to introduce education for sustainable consumption in the formal education sector.

■ E-textile toolbox (Vietnam and India)

Partner organizations from Asia and Europe have joined hands to develop an on-line toolbox to help make textile production more efficient, reduce production costs, improve product quality and achieve a better environmental performance. The integrated toolbox consists of an on-line capacity building module to acquire competitive knowledge, a performance management tool and a catalogue of technical solutions and examples of their application.

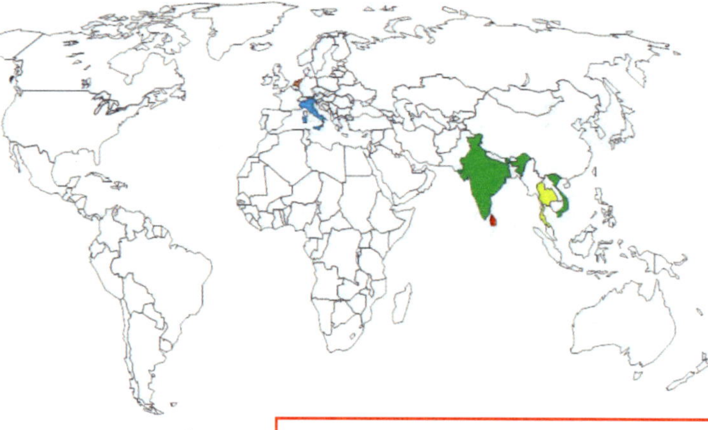

■ Food and Beverage Industry (Sri Lanka)

The SWITCH ASIA programme focuses on sustainable consumption and production (SCP) and directly contributes to sustainable growth and the fight against poverty in Asia. The Food & Beverage industry is a very important sector of Sri Lankan economy that contributes around 10% of GDP and generate an annual export revenue of US$1.4 bn. This project, under SWITCH ASIA, improves the environmental performance of the Food & Beverage sector through promotion of best practices of sustainable production among Small and Medium Enterprises.

■ Sustainable livelihoods (Asia and the Pacific)

Green Growth is a policy focus for Asia and the Pacific that emphasizes ecologically sustainable economic progress to foster low-carbon, socially inclusive development. There has been an increasing number of requests for capacity development assistance from governments in the region. To meet such needs, the UN Economic and Social Commission for Asia and the Pacific (ESCAP) has designed a unique training package on Green Growth policy tools for the area. This tool has evolved to emphasize the Sustainable Livelihoods approach (SLA). ESCAP's Training of Trainers (TOT) Programme works to assist in building individual and organizational capabilities to ensure Green Growth goals can be defined and realized at the national level. By engaging internal and external expertise in trainings, the programme increases its value-added. Training is targeted towards middle-level government managers, ministerial officials, private-sector decision makers, NGOs, academics and other actors, i.e. all stakeholders involved in the country's transition to green growth. The method emphasizes new forms of training such as group exercises, brainstorming, case studies and role playing amongst others.

CONSUMER-CITIZENS

National Geographic and GlobeScan have launched a quantitative consumer study of 17,000 consumers in a total of 17 countries (14 in 2008) asking questions about such behavior as energy use and conservation, transportation choices, food sources, the relative use of green products versus traditional products, attitudes towards the environment and sustainability, and knowledge of environmental issues. These are the behaviors that were most critical to investigate based on a group of international experts. A composite measure of environmentally sustainable consumption called the Greendex was developed to score each respondent based on the consumption patterns s/he reports in the survey, and compares average scores by country for 17 countries.

The Greendex is composed of 65 measurements of consumer behavior in the areas above. Each respondent earns a score reflecting the environmental impact of his or her consumption patterns within each, leading to corresponding "sub-indices". The overall Greendex score is a number out of 100, based on their performance within the sub-indices. The highest score was 59.5 out of a 100 for India and the lowest 43.7 for the USA.

The top-scoring consumers of 2009 (where higher scores are "greener") are in the developing economies of India, Brazil and China. Argentina and South Korea, both new additions to the survey, are virtually tied for fourth, followed by Mexico, Hungary and Russia. Ranks ninth through thirteenth, the latter a three-way tie, are all occupied by European countries, as well as Australia in twelfth. Japanese, U.S. and Canadian consumers score lowest.

An increase was reported in environmentally friendly consumer behavior in 13 of the 14 countries surveyed in both 2008 and 2009. Survey results suggest that both cost considerations and environmental concerns may have motivated consumers to adopt more environmentally sustainable behavior over the past two years.

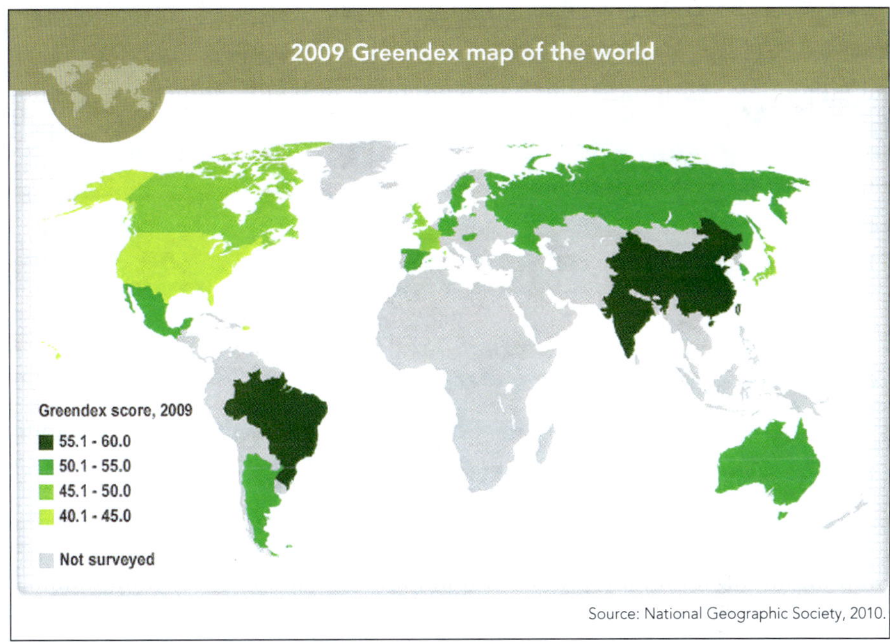

Source: National Geographic Society, 2010.

> **"Current global consumption patterns are unsustainable…it is becoming apparent that efficiency gains and technological advances alone will not be sufficient to bring global consumption to a sustainable level; changes will also be required to consumer lifestyles, including the ways in which consumers choose and use products and services."**
>
> — *Sustainable Consumption Facts and Trends from a Business Perspective, World Business Council for Sustainable Development, 2008*

PERL (Global)

The Partnership for Education and Research about Responsible Living (PERL) is a network of about 100 higher education institutions from 40 countries. It is based on six years of experience under the Consumer Citizenship Network mainly in Europe. It started in 2009 and will run till 2012. PERL is a partnership that aims to examine and stimulate the incorporation of sustainability in daily actions, including consumption choices, and the creation of sustainable and responsible lifestyles by:

• Researching social innovation and responsibility;
• Giving visibility to creative communities that collaboratively invent new ways of living;
• Promoting education for sustainable consumption;
• Stimulating consumer citizenship;
• Developing teaching methods and materials;
• Providing references and guidance;
• Producing recommendations for sustainable lifestyles and education for sustainable consumption.

Already teacher training modules, courses and educational toolkits have been developed to help trainers and individuals to understand and communicate on sustainable lifestyle.

Carrotmob (Global)

Carrotmob is a type of consumer activism in which businesses compete at how socially responsible they can be. Then a network of consumers spends money to support whichever business makes the strongest offer. The goal is to harness consumer power to make it possible for the most socially-responsible business practices to be the most profitable choices. It is the opposite of a boycott. Since 2008 over 50 Carrotmob events have been organized worldwide.

Nudging (Global)

Nudging is about making it easier to make the sustainable choice. The default choice is the sustainable one, and consumers have to opt-in to the unsustainable one. One example is moving plastic bags at the grocery store under the counter and training cashiers to wait until they are asked to give a bag, instead of offering them automatically and having them in view. This simple change has proven to reduce significantly the number of bags used. Nudging also changes what people perceive as acceptable behavior — in many areas it is embarrassing to ask or be seen with a plastic bag.

The 10:10 (The United Kingdom)

The 10-10 campaign is an ambitious project to unite every sector of society behind one simple idea: all commit to reduce CO_2 emissions by 10% in 2010, then work together to make it happen. The target was set based on studies that showed that 10% reduction a year starting this year is the kind of target that will give us the best chance of a safe future for our children and grandchildren. Already, 60,000 people, 2,300 businesses, 500 schools, colleges and universities, 1,300 organisations have signed on in the UK. And the campaign is rapidly spreading around the world with campaigns already up and running in Ireland, Norway, France, Portugal, Ghana, and the Netherlands.

Sustainable Connections (United States)

Sustainable Connections works as the local forum where businesses come together to transform and model an economy built on sustainable practices. For example, it supports a community of innovators in green building, sustainable agriculture and renewable energy. Since its start in 2002 Sustainable Connections has grown to 650+ local, independently owned business members and an annual budget nearing $1m. Sustainable Connections worked with the city of Bellingham, Washington and, in 2009, the National Resources Defense Council named Bellingham the #1 small city in urban progress toward sustainability.

LivingSmart (Australia)

Living Smart is a program offering information on how to reduce greenhouse gas emissions at home and in daily travel. The program works with selected communities to achieve savings for households and large reductions in greenhouse gas emissions. The program aims to reduce carbon dioxide emissions 1.5 tons per household a year. (Australians on average emit 14 tons per household.) This will save participants up to 10 percent in their gas, electric, water, and petroleum bills.

Slow Food (Italy)

The slow food movement challenges consumers to think about how consumption choices form part of a interdependent network within a social economy — the pleasures of food preparation and consumption among friends and family helps develop social and cultural capital. An important component of the Slow Food movement is the commitment to educate children about the origins and taste of food — to help them to have a connection to the food they eat. The Slow Food movement has its origins in the 1980s in Italy and currently has 65,000 members in 42 countries.

Eco-Action Points (Japan)

Since 2008, the Ministry of the Environment has promoted the Eco-Action Point model projects, in which citizens can earn points in exchange for their environment friendly actions — including purchase of energy-saving products/services — and redeem those points for a range of awards, such as train tickets, daily goods and donations to help protect the environment. There are three nationwide Eco-Action Point model projects and nine local projects.

Business and Industry (Global)

The Responsible Care® Global Charter addresses sustainable development and public health issues with respect to the use of chemical products. It highlights the industry's commitment to continuous improvement and greater transparency in environmental, health and safety performance. Responsible Care is currently implemented by 53 industry associations.

NGOs / Trade Unions (Global)

About 10 years ago, various trade unions and social justice and environmental NGOs worldwide started the international flower campaign. The aim of the campaign is twofold: to improve conditions for workers in the flower industry and to stimulate sustainable production of cut flowers. The collaboration between unions and NGOs resulted in the International Code of Conduct for the Production of Cut Flowers (ICC). The standards of this Code are based on International Labour Organisation criteria and international conventions and/or treaties. The International Code of Conduct has already been accepted by the international industry united in Union Fleurs. The International Code of Conduct provides a concise statement of minimum labour and human rights.

The joint efforts of industry, NGOs and trade unions represent the most effective way to improve working conditions and sustainable production. An independent body, established to provide independent verification of compliance with the code and to assist companies to implement the code, will provide an auditable checklist of practices and conditions that are consistent with the standards set forth in the code.

Farmers (Peru)

Farmer members of the National Coffee Board (Junta Nacional del Café) of Peru are currently working on the implementation of sustainable agricultural practices. These are put in place in 30% of the total area under coffee managed by the Board and include the implementation of soil conservation practices and reforestation projects that increase productivity and reduce pressure on forests.

Business and Industry (Global)

The air transport industry is exploring opportunities offered by technology such as revolutionary new plane designs, new composite lightweight materials, radical new engine advances, and the development of sustainable biofuels for aviation. Airlines will spend $1.5 trillion on new aircraft by 2020. Some 5,500 aircraft will be replaced by 2020, or 27% of the total fleet. With adoption of these new technologies there could be a 21% reduction in CO_2 emissions compared to business as usual.

Youth (Mali)

As part of a decade-long initiative of the United Nations Development Programme (UNDP) and United Nations Industrial Development Organization (UNIDO), the multi-functional platform project provides decentralized energy to rural villages in response to requests from local women's associations in Mali. The small size and dispersed locations of villages in Mali make off-grid decentralized mechanical and electric energy supply the only viable option. The multi-functional platform is a 10-horse-power diesel engine that was purposefully designed to take into account multiple end uses for energy in rural economies.

Farmers (Albania))

In the face of severe erosion threats, Albanian farmers have identified and implemented good agricultural practices to maintain soil productivity, conserve water and lower production costs. These practices include adequate crop rotation, intercropping, zero or minimum tillage, mulching, effective irrigation systems and rain collection systems, selection of resistant varieties, composting and biological pest and disease control. In order to stop further land degradation, the development of agricultural good practices includes afforestation, the setting up of barriers to protect the arable land, and the improvement of irrigation systems.

Women (Bangladesh)

Women in Bangladesh Make Battery-Powered Lamps. The project aims at improving the lighting and indoor air quality of rural households by replacing the traditional kerosene lamps with modern fluorescent battery-powered lamps, which have a reduced risk of fire and do not give off smoke and other emissions harmful to human health. Funded by the World Bank Energy Sector Management Programme (ESMAP), it has been running on the remote island of Char Montaz in the south of Bangladesh since 1999.

NGOs (Southern Africa)

Farming for Energy, for Better Livelihoods in Southern Africa (FELISA) is both a concept and a project that promotes the production and use of bioenergy, particularly biodiesel. With FELISA, it is projected that countries in the Southern African Development Community (SADC) can satisfy a significant portion of liquid fuel needs, hence making them less dependent on foreign exchange, by allocating less than 10% of their cropland to energy crops.

Collaborative Labeling and Appliance Standards Program (US)

Energy efficiency standards and labels (S&L) for appliances, equipment and lighting are a cost-effective means to help countries limit energy demand. CLASP seeks to serve as the primary international resource for policymakers and practitioners of energy efficiency standards and labeling for residential, commercial and industrial equipment and lighting worldwide. It promotes the cost-effective adoption of S&L throughout the world. Since its initiation in 1999 CLASP has supported the development of 24 new minimum energy performance standards and/or energy labels, and has provided S&L technical assistance to over 50 countries.

Refrigerants, Naturally! (US)

Refrigerants, Naturally! is a global initiative of companies committed to combat climate change and ozone layer depletion by substituting harmful fluorinated gases (such as CFCs, HCFCs and HFCs) with natural refrigerants. The goal is to promote a shift in the point-of-sale cooling technology in the food and drink, food service and retail sectors towards natural refrigerants with a low or zero Global Warming Potential.

Methane to Markets (US)

The Methane to Markets Partnership is an international initiative that advances cost-effective, near-term methane recovery and use as a clean energy source. The goal of the Partnership is to reduce global methane emissions in order to enhance economic growth, strengthen energy security, improve air quality, improve industrial safety, and reduce emissions of greenhouse gases. The Partnership currently focuses on four sources of methane emissions: agriculture (animal waste management), coal mines, landfills and oil and gas systems. The Partnership grew from 14 Partners in 2004 to 31 in 2009 and its supported projects are reducing emissions by more than 27 $MTCO_2e$ per year.

Water Improvements (Philippines)

In the 1990s water and wastewater services in Manila were unsafe, unreliable and most residents were under-served, while others had no access to the systems at all. In 1995, the Philippine government enacted legislation which allowed Manila's water agency to enter into a public-private partnership and agreement was made with Maynilad Water Services, Inc. As of 2009, there were a total 790,000 households in Manila served by Maynilad, an increase of approximately 75% since the concession agreement. Of that number, approximately 60% have access to 24-hour water service, while an estimated 74% receive water at 7 pounds per square inch (psi), or strong pressure. The numbers represent a significant increase from the previous numbers, 32% with 24-hour service and 45% with 7 psi, seen under the prior ownership (the government).

Sustainable Water (Somalia)

The newly rehabilitated water system in Berbera, Somalia, is managed under the public-private partnership approach, which involves the community, the Water Authority and the private sector in ensuring sustainable service delivery. The water board, which was established specifically for this project, represents the various stakeholders and helps monitor and improve the water management system. UNICEF and the European Union introduced this approach in Somalia in 1997. Since then, several other key donors have come on board to support similar projects. Today, 10 such projects are being implemented to bring safe water to Somali communities across the country.

The SEED Initiative (Kenya)

The global SEED Initiative nurtures and publicizes exceptional, entrepreneurial multi-stakeholder partnerships for locally-led sustainable development. The initiative focuses on 'business as unusual' — innovative action delivering real solutions through project cooperation among small and large businesses, local and international NGOs, women's groups, labour organisations, public authorities and UN agencies, and others working in the field of sustainable development.

V. NEW TECHNOLOGIES AND FINANCE

Government policies contribute importantly to setting the incentive and regulatory framework to induce a shift towards sustainable patterns of consumption and production. Often, behavioral responses of consumers or managerial changes of producers can achieve significant results. Nevertheless, to make the major changes needed in coming decades will require more. It will require development of new environmentally sound technologies as well as a much faster scaling up of both current and yet-to-be developed technologies. Technology development and scale-up in turn require significant financing to make the necessary investments.

New technologies

The most significant technological advance of the past generation has been the very rapid growth and increasing penetration of Information and Communication Technologies (ICT) in both developed and developing countries. While manufacturing ICT equipment produces sizeable new material flows and using ICT generates significant energy demand (still largely supplied by fossil fuels), ICT has at the same time made possible significant improvements in resource and energy efficiency and reductions in waste. By one estimate (see figure), the carbon mitigation opportunities made possible by ICT applications outweigh the ICT sector's own carbon footprint by a factor of five.

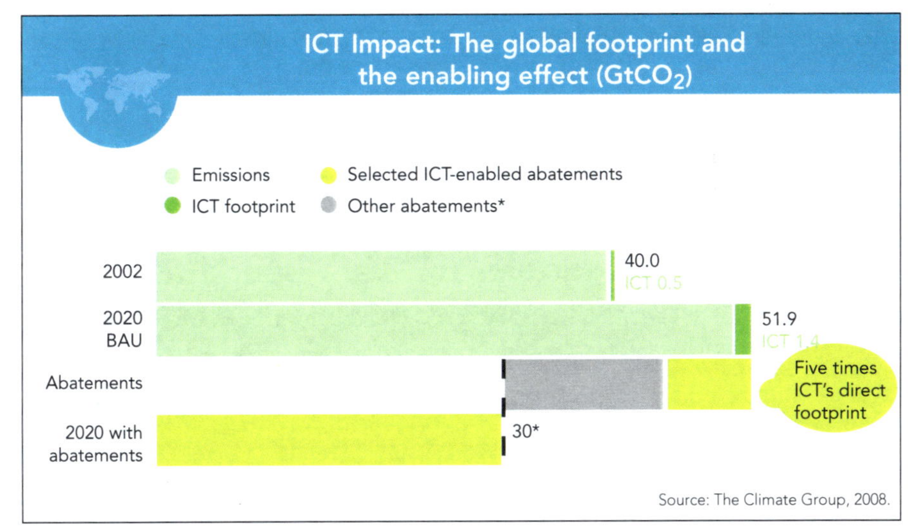

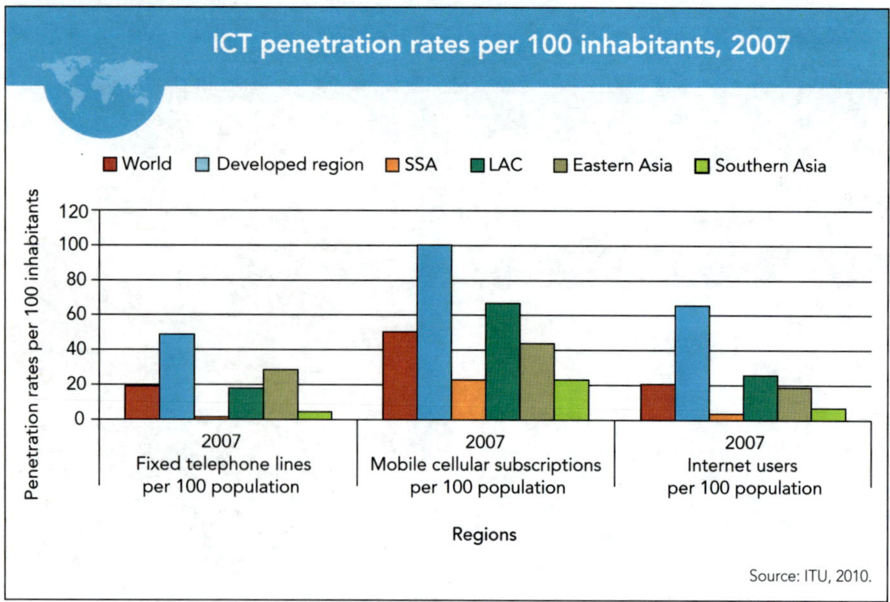

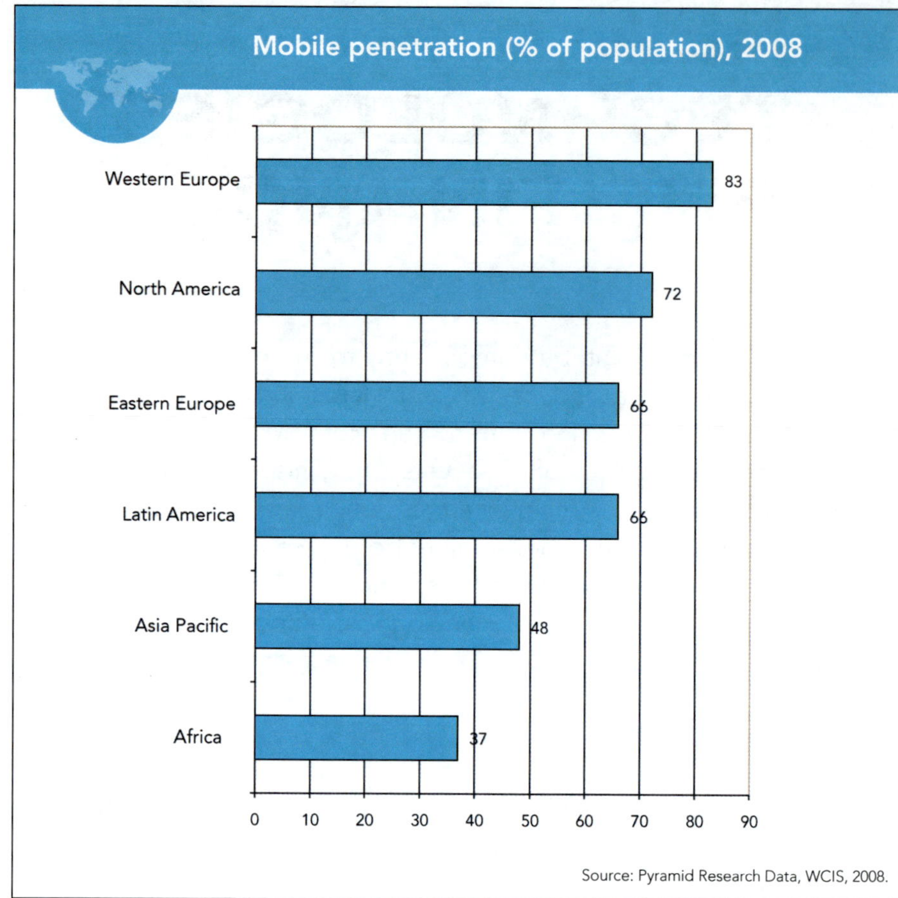

ICT — and in particular mobile telephony — represents a case of technology leapfrogging which has brought affordable communications to rural areas of the developing world, leaping over fixed-line phone technology. Sub-Saharan Africa's and Southern Asia's negligible fixed-line coverage but significant mobile cellular coverage (see figure) illustrates this well.

> **As the world economy begins to recover from one of the worst economic crises in decades, information and communication technologies (ICT) are bound to play an increasingly prominent role as a key enabler of renewed and sustainable growth, given that it has become an essential element of the infrastructure underpinning competitive economies.**
>
> — *WEF, The Global Information Technology Report 2009–2010.*

Mobile phones (increasingly wifi capable) have extended a range of services to the rural poor, such as e-banking (including microfinance and remittance management), on-the-spot agricultural information and advice (e.g. weather, pests, prices) and remote access to medical information and advice, including veterinary medicine.

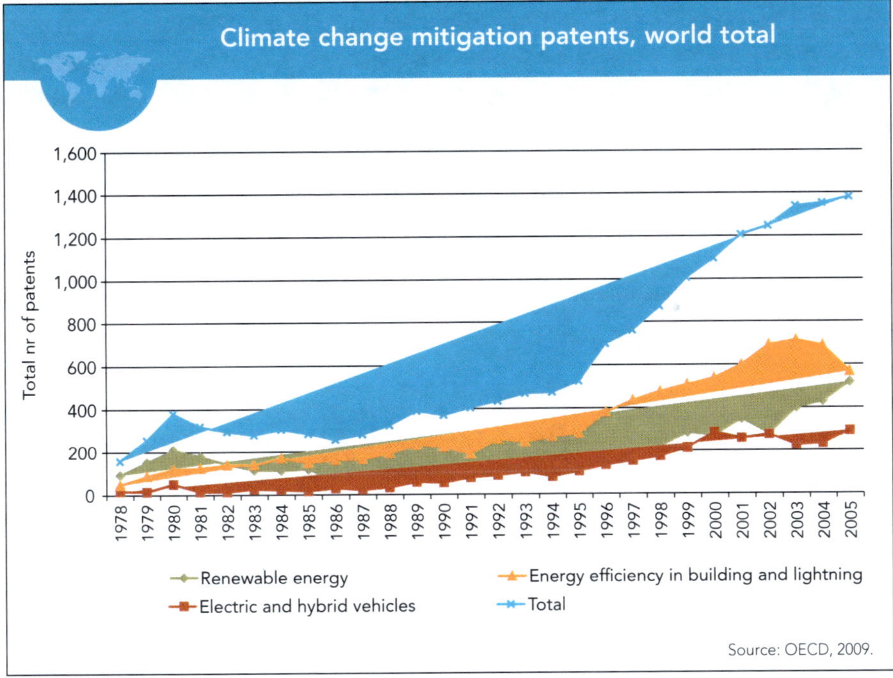

Patent filings and awards show an acceleration in recent years of innovation in climate change mitigation technologies, with renewable energy and energy efficiency in buildings and lighting roughly on a par in numbers of patents issued.

Ecological footprints of new and emerging technologies are still uncertain. Industrial biotechnology has a number of potential applications for enhancing sustainability. For instance, enzymes have been developed that reduce the heat of water needed to wash clothes; others are being developed to convert cellulosic biomass from agricultural waste or energy crops into fermentable sugars for producing bio-ethanol; still others to reduce nitrogen emissions from animal farming.

Energy savings from nanotechnologies are expected to be significant. For example, they will enable: solar cells that are produced at reduced costs and provide higher efficiency; light-weight transportation components that improve fuel economy in automobiles and trucks; more efficient lighting (i.e., LEDs) at homes and offices; and better performing catalysts/ separations/ materials technologies that enhance the energy efficiency of manufacturing[9].

On the other hand, their environmental and health impacts are still imperfectly understood. Potential occupational and public exposure to manufactured nanoparticles will increase dramatically in the near future due to the ability of nanomaterial to improve the quality and performance of many common consumer products as well as the development of medical therapies and tests which use manufactured nanoparticles[10]. Yet, there is still a paucity of information on nanoparticle toxicology and exposure assessments and they are also very resource intensive.

Finance

Finance is needed both to develop new technologies for more sustainable consumption and production, and to build the infrastructure and plant and equipment to realize more sustainable consumption and production patterns and make more sustainable products.

Of particular importance in the future will be the development of a low-carbon energy infrastructure and provision of low-carbon energy and transportation services in developing countries to support strong economic growth and social development.

The following figures provide a snapshot of trends in new investment in renewable energy technologies in particular, but also in other technologies which can help reduce carbon footprints while improving energy access.

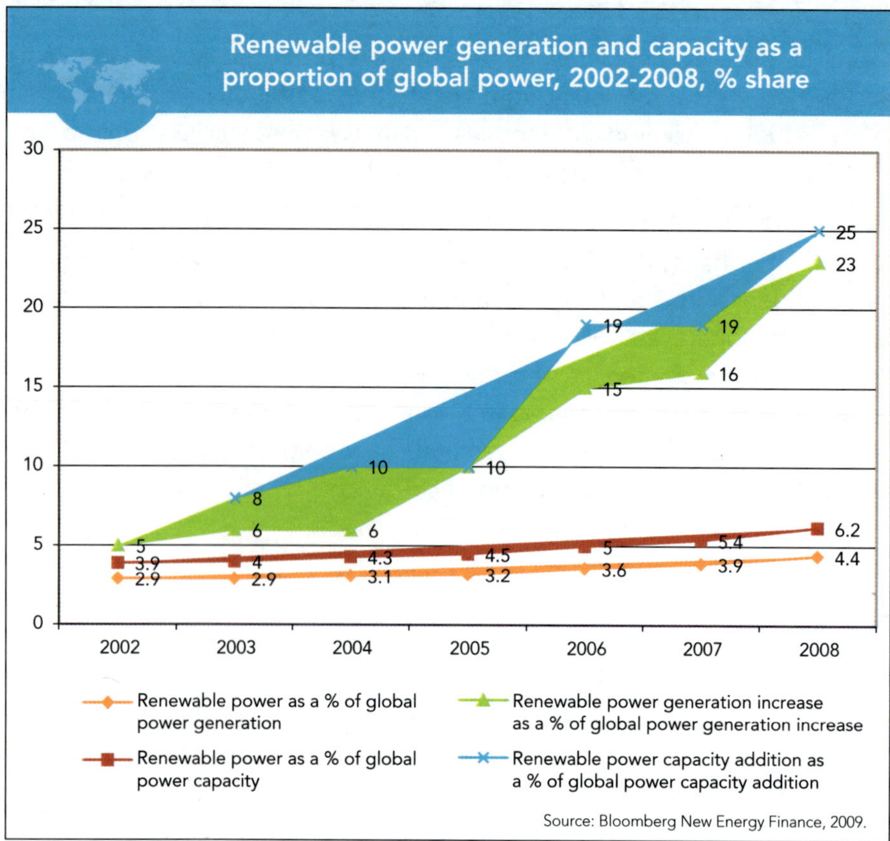

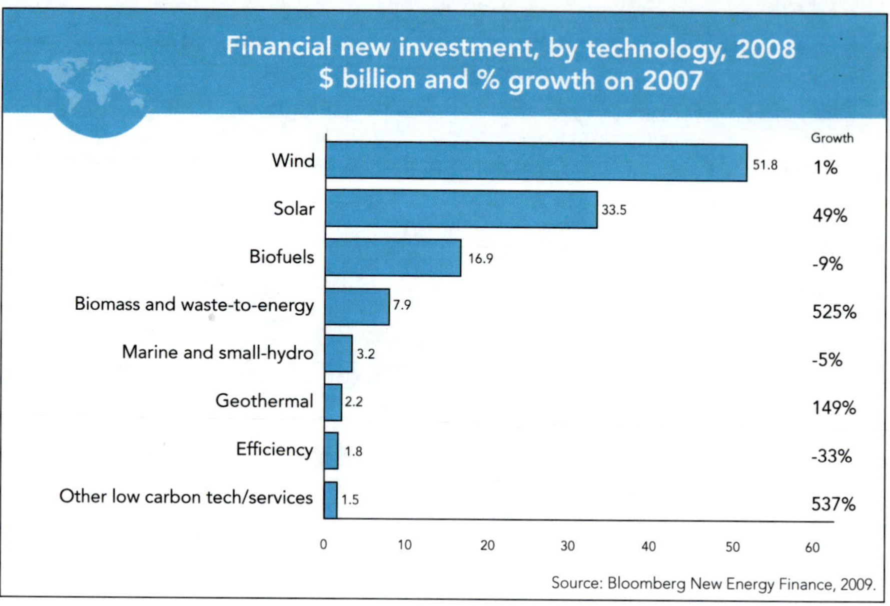

While renewable energy remains a small share of global capacity in the power sector, its share of added capacity in that sector has been growing steeply during the past decade, reaching one-quarter of power capacity additions as of 2008.

Developing countries' share of total global financial investment in renewables increased to 31% in 2008, from 26% in 2007. China led investment in Asia, with $15.6 billion of new investment, mostly in new wind projects, and some biomass plants. Investment in India grew 12% to $3.7billion in 2008, of which asset finance represented $3.2 billion, up 36%. Brazil accounted for almost all renewable energy investment in Latin America in 2008, receiving $10.8 billion, up 7% from 2007[11].

Socially and environmentally screened investments have become more popular over the past decade, as evident from data on "responsible investments (RI)". The RI penetration is expected to reach between 15 to 20 percent of total Assets Under Management (AUM) or around $26.5 trillion by 2015. If the RI market enters a proliferation phase the global RI growth rate could rise to 30 percent per year. Europe — especially Switzerland and the UK — will drive much of this growth. With its growth rate of 28 percent per annum, the European RI market is expected to reach $14.2 trillion, overtaking the US RI market. Currently the largest RI market, the US, is expected to grow to $9.5 trillion by 2015.

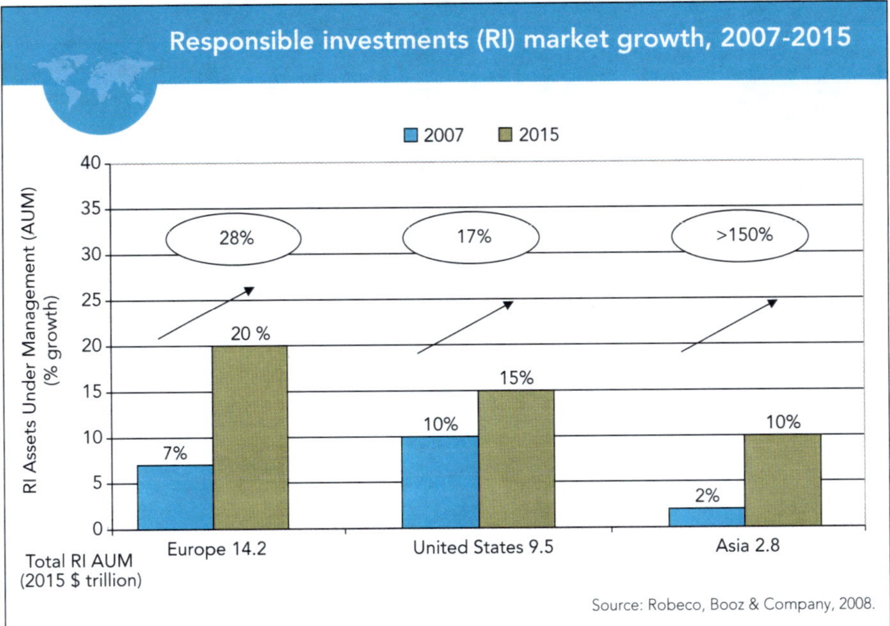

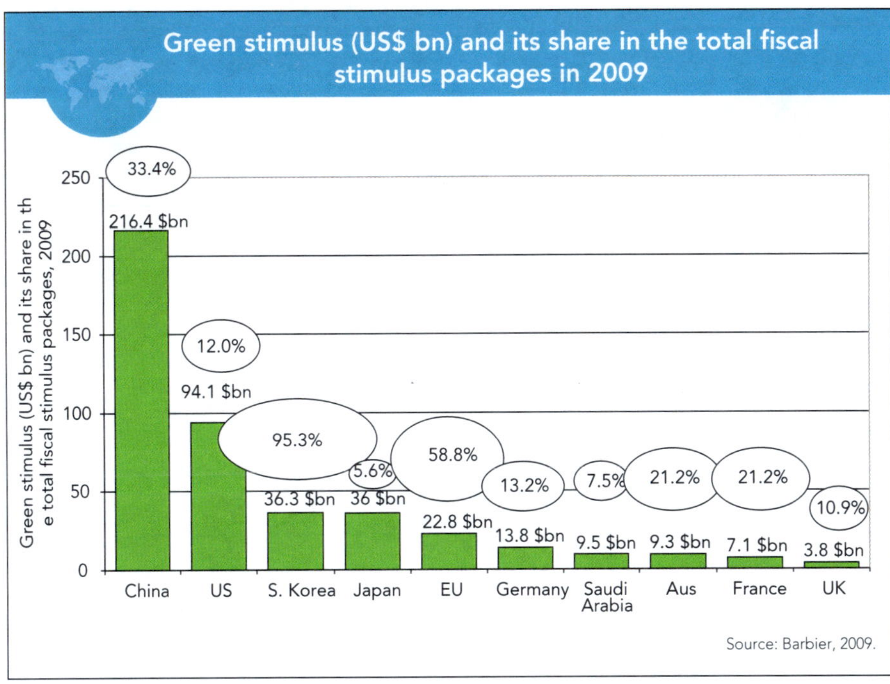

Socially responsible investing has been depressed, along with other investments, by the ongoing global recession. Clean energy investment funds have also suffered the effects of the ongoing uncertainty in the global climate regime following the inconclusive Copenhagen climate change negotiations. On the other hand, government spending on "green" investments has received a significant boost during the recession, with substantial portions of stimulus packages in many countries earmarked for environmentally sound investments.

Socially and environmentally screened investments (Socially responsible investment, or SRI) and assets managed according to environmental, social and governance (ESG) criteria represent an increasing share of assets under management, reaching 10% in the US, 7% in Europe and 2% in Asia in 2007. Growth is expected to continue in Europe and the US and to explode in Asia to 150% to bring SRI penetration to 10% by 2015. Total assets under management that are socially and environmentally screened are expected to reach $26.5 trillion by 2015. The UN Principles for Responsible Investment have attracted 640 signatories with combined assets under management of $14 trillion. The trend is toward ESG that, instead of or in addition to screening out undesirable corporate citizens, selects leading companies in their sectors to drive continuous improvement.

The recent increase in renewable energy investment and green stimulus spending has not been limited to the developed countries. Emerging economies play an increasingly prominent role in these technologies and sectors. China registered the largest absolute amount of green stimulus spending, while Republic Korea registered the largest green share of its stimulus. In the case of renewable energy, Brazil is a world leader in production of biofuels, while China and India both have sizeable installed capacity of wind and solar PV.

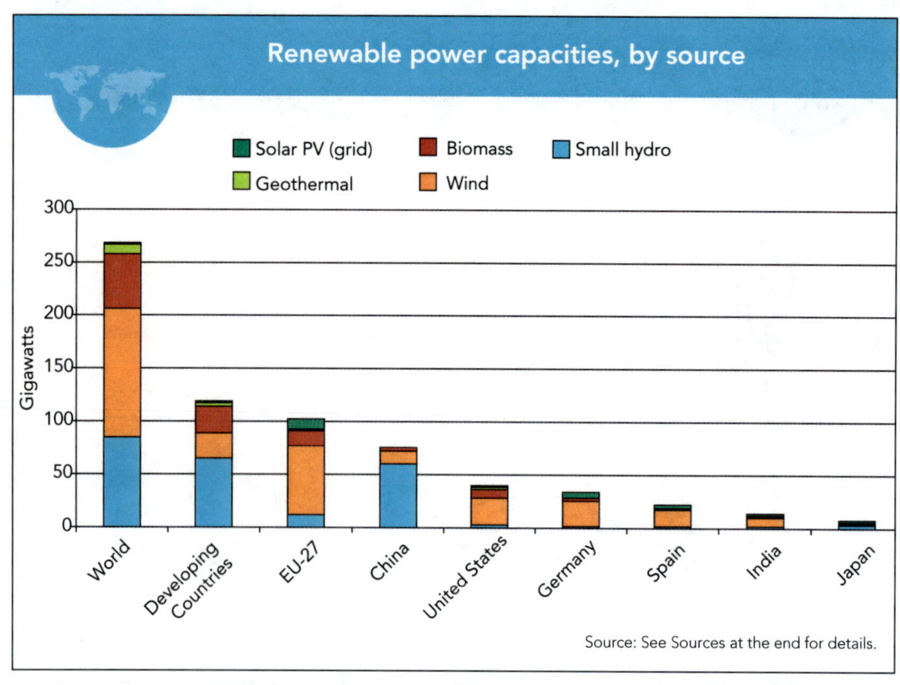

Renewable power capacities, by source
Solar PV (grid)
Biomass
Small hydro
Geothermal
Wind
Gigawatts
300
250
200
150
100
50
0
World
Developing Countries
EU-27
China
United States
Germany
Spain
India
Japan
Source: See Sources at the end for details.

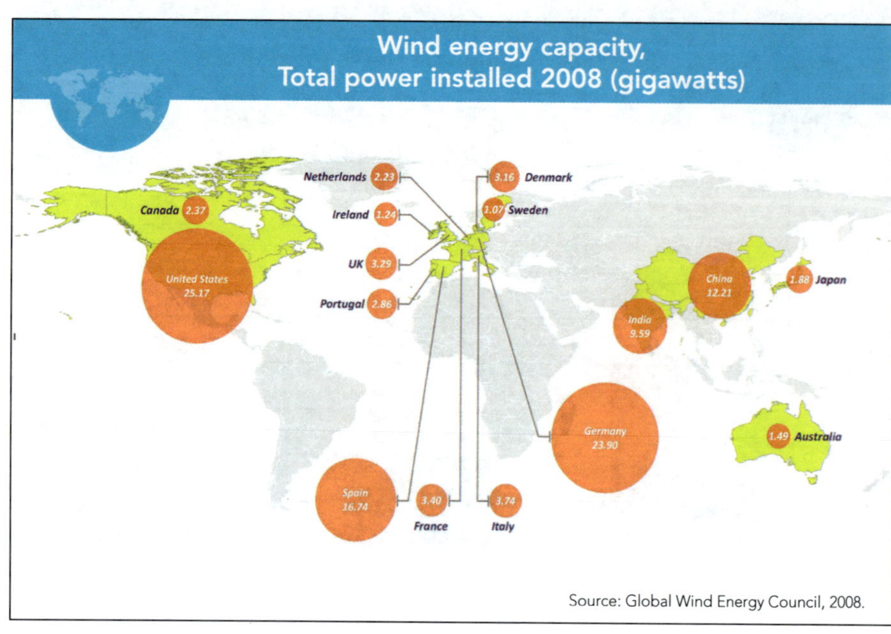

Wind energy capacity,
Total power installed 2008 (gigawatts)
Canada 2.37
United States 25.17
Netherlands 2.23
Ireland 1.24
UK 3.25
Portugal 2.86
Denmark 3.16
Sweden 1.07
Spain 16.74
France 3.40
Italy 3.74
Germany 23.90
India 9.59
China 12.21
Japan 1.88
Australia 1.49
Source: Global Wind Energy Council, 2008.

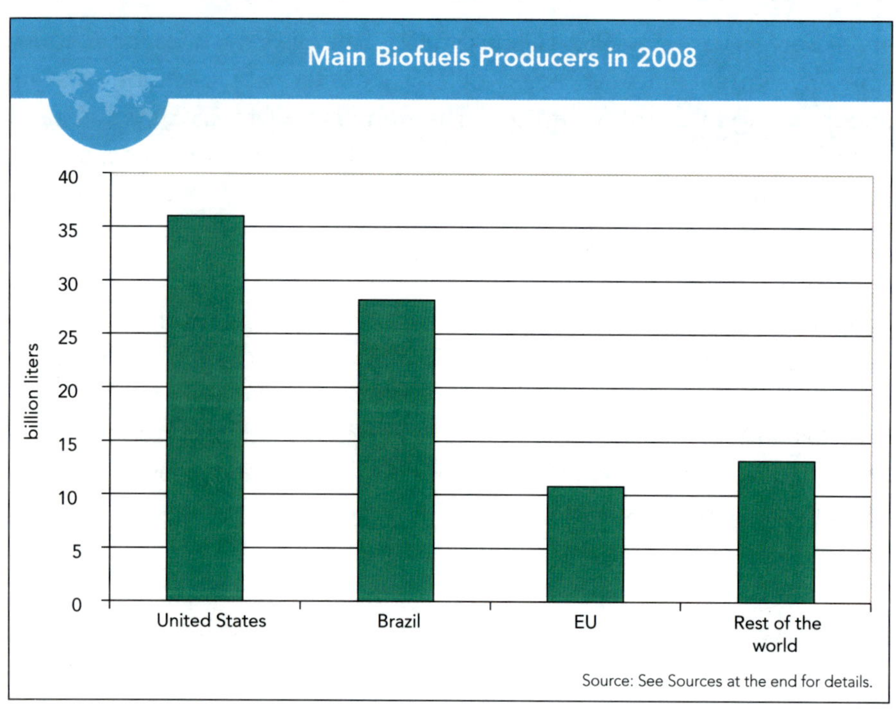

Main Biofuels Producers in 2008
billion liters
40
35
30
25
20
15
10
5
0
United States
Brazil
EU
Rest of the world
Source: See Sources at the end for details.

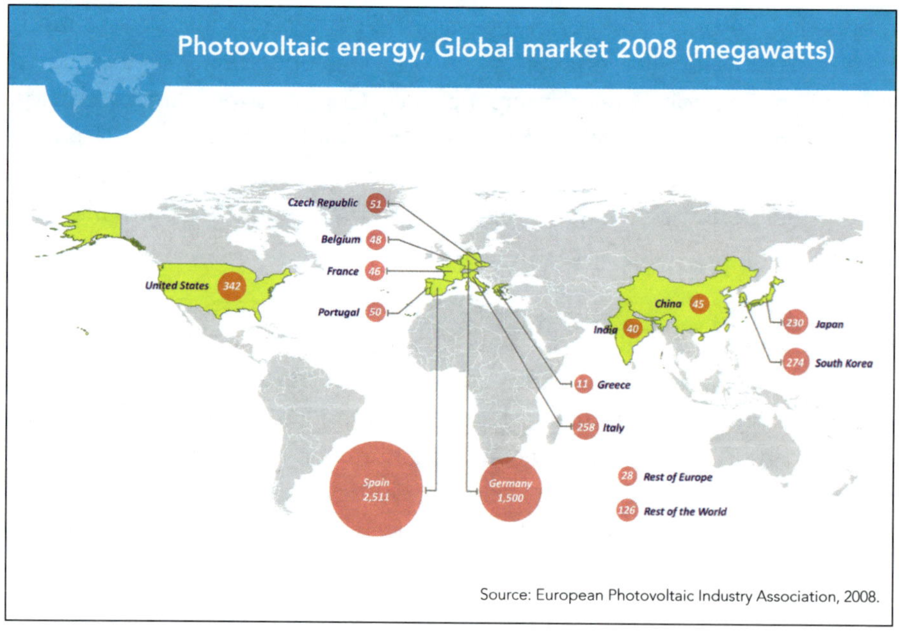

Photovoltaic energy, Global market 2008 (megawatts)
Czech Republic 51
Belgium 48
France 46
Portugal 50
United States 342
India 40
China 45
Japan 230
South Korea 274
Greece 11
Italy 258
Spain 2,511
Germany 1,500
Rest of Europe 28
Rest of the World 126
Source: European Photovoltaic Industry Association, 2008.

SOURCES AND NOTES
FOR MAPS AND GRAPHS

Trends in Resource Use

SERI Global Material Flow Database. 2010 Version. See www.materialflows.net.

International Monetary Fund, International Financial Statistics, 2010. See www.imfstatistics.org.

Stresses on Ecosystems

Rockstrom J. et al. 2009. A safe operating space for humanity Nature 461: 472-475 (September) 2009. Published online September 23, 2009.

Boden, T.A., G. Marland, and R.J. Andres. 2009. Global, Regional, and National Fossil-Fuel CO_2 Emissions. Carbon Dioxide Information Analysis Center, Oak Ridge National Laboratory, U.S. Department of Energy, Oak Ridge, Tenn., U.S.A. doi 10.3334/CDIAC/00001

IUCN Red List version 2010.1: Table 1, 2010. Note: Estimated total number of vertebrate species 62 305; invertebrate species 1 305 250; plant species 321 212 and Fungi & Protists species 1 740 330.

Food and Agriculture Organization of the United Nations, ResourceSTAT database, 2010 (Accessed 24 March 2010)

UNEP/GRID-Arendal, Estimated total reactive nitrogen deposition from the atmosphere (wet and dry) in 1860, early 1990s, and projected for 2050, UNEP/GRID-Arendal Maps and Graphics Library, http://maps.grida.no/go/graphic/estimated-total-reactive-nitrogen-deposition-from-the-atmosphere-wet-and-dry-in-1860-early-1990s-and (Accessed 25 March 2010)

WWF, 2008. Living Planet Report 2008, Gland, Switzerland.

Stabilizing Water Tables," Chapter 6 in Lester R. Brown, Outgrowing the Earth: The Food Security Challenge in an Age of Falling Water Tables and Rising Temperatures (New York: W.W. Norton & Company, 2005), pp. 106-107. Updated by Elizabeth Mygatt, E

Hoekstra, A.Y. and Chapagain, A.K. (2007) Water footprints of nations: water use by people as a function of their consumption pattern, Water Resources Management. 21(1): 35-48.

OECD. Statistics portal, 2010 (Accessed 2 March 2010)

Drivers of Changing Production and Consumption Patterns

Global footprint network (2008) Global footprint atlas 2009. UNDP (2008)

Global footprint network (2009). Footprint Atlas 2009 p.25.

Goldman Sachs 2008. Expanding Middle — The Expanding World Middle Class and falling global inequality.

International Energy Agency (IEA) Statistics Division. 2007. Energy Balances of OECD Countries (2008 edition) and Energy Balances of Non-OECD Countries (2007 edition). Paris: IEA.

World Bank, World Development Indicators 2009.

United Nations, Population Division, World Population Prospects: The 2008 Revision, http://esa.un.org/unpp/

Hertwich E. and Peters G.P. Carbon Footprint of Nations: A Global, Trade-Linked Analysis. Environ. Sci. Technol. 2009, 43, 6414–6420. Note: Production-based emissions are defined as total emissions generated within a country, and consumption-based emissions as emissions generated through the production of goods and services that are consumed within a country regardless of the production site locations. The differences between production-based and consumption-based emissions are attributed to the CO_2 emissions embodied in the goods moving across the national border through trade. A fully coupled multiregional input-output (MRIO) model using the Global Trade Analysis Project (GTAP) database supplemented with data on CO_2 emissions and non-CO_2 greenhouse gas emissions was used. The sources and sinks of land use, land use change, and forestry (LULUCF) were not included in the analysis because of the difficulty in allocating to economic activity. As LULUCF is the dominant source of emissions in many countries, care should be taken to note that these results only consider the emissions of fossil fuels and process emissions.

Policy and Voluntary Responses

Fairtrade Labelling Organizations International. Fair trade leading the way. Annual Report 2008-09. 2009. Page 22.

United Nations Global Compact, 2009. Global Compact Annual Review 2008.

ISO Survey 2008.

Global Reporting Initiative. GRI Reports List, 2010.

National Geographic Society., 2010. http://www.nationalgeographic.com/greendex/

New Technologies and Finance

The Climate Group (2008) SMART 2020: Enabling the low carbon economy in the information age, London, p15.

International Telecommunications Union Statistics, 2010.

Pyramid Research Data, Q3 2008; World Cellular Information Service online database, accessed October 2009.

OECD Patent database 2010.

Bloomberg New Energy Finance, 2009. Note: Excluding Large hydro power.

Bloomberg New Energy Finance, 2009.

Note: Financial new investment contains 3 asset classes: 1) VC/PE investment at the company level; 2) asset finance into building projects (any power producing clean energy project or biofuels refinery); and 3) public market transactions to raise equity, such as IPOs. New investment volume adjusts for re-invested equity. Total values include estimates for undisclosed deals.

Robeco, Booz & Company. Responsible Investing: A Paradigm Shift. From Niche to Mainstream. The Netherlands, 2008. Note: AUM as % of total AUM; bubble refers to RI Growth 2007-2015 p.a.

Barbier, Edward B. Global Governance: the G20 and a Global Green New Deal. Economics: the Open-Access, Open Assessment E-Journal. Discussion Paper Nr. 2009-38 | August 21, 2009 | http://www.economics journal.org/economics/discussionpapers/2009-38.

GWEC 2009, WWEA 2009, and Spanish Wind Energy Association; PV News/Prometheus Institute unpublished figures for 2008; European Photovoltaic Industries Association; Systèmes Solaires Eur'Observer 190, March 2009; news reports; expert estimates from report contributors.; International Energy Agency (IEA) Renewables Information 2008 (for OECD biomass power capacity); submissions from Renewable Energy Policy Network for the 21st century (2009). Renewables. Global status- report contributors.

F.O. Licht, World Ethanol and Biofuels Report; Argentina from Argentine Biofuels and Hydrogen Association; Brazil from Brazil. Note: Small amounts, on the order of a few megawatts, are designated by "~0."

Reference Center on Biomass (CENBIO).Brazil transportation fuel share from Clean Edge, Clean Energy Trends 2009 (San Francisco: March 2009). Note: Ethanol numbers are for fuel ethanol only. Table ranking by total biofuels. U.S. and Brazil ethanol figures rounded to nearest billion liters.

Global Wind Energy Council, Global Wind 2008 Report.

European Photovoltaic Industry Association, 2008, Global Market Outlook for Photovoltaics until 2013.

REFERENCES

1   World Development Indicators 2009, World Bank.

2   Millennium Ecosystem Assessment, 2005, Ecosystems and Human Well-being: Synthesis. WRI: Island Press, Washington, DC. milleniumassessment.org.

3   J.N. Galloway et al (2008). "Transformation of the Nitrogen Cycle: Recent Trends, Questions, and Potential Solutions." Science 16 May 2008, and R.A. Duce t al (2008). "Impacts of Atmospheric Anthropogenic Nitrogen on the Open Ocean." Science 16 May 2008.

4   R. L. Mulvaney, S. A. Khan and T. R. Ellsworth (2009), Synthetic Nitrogen Fertilizers Deplete Soil Nitrogen: A Global Dilemma for Sustainable Cereal Production, Journal of Environmental Quality, 38:2295-2314.

5   WWF. 2008. Living Planet Report 2008. WWF: Gland Switzerland.

6   OECD 2008. Consumption, Production and Technology. Chapter 1 in OECD Environmental Outlook to 2030. Paris, OECD.

7   Fairtrade Labelling Organizations International. Fair trade leading the way. Annual Report 2008-09. 2009.

8   Global Reporting Initiative. Principles and Guidelines. See www.globalreporting.org.

9   U.S. Department of Energy (2007), Nanomanufacturing for Energy Efficiency. Workshop Report, December.

10   K. L. Dreher (2004), Health and Environmental Impact of Nanotechnology: Toxicological Assessment of Manufactured Nano-particles, Toxicological Sciences, 77, 3-5.

11   UNEP and New Energy Finance (2009), Global Trends in Sustainable Energy Investment 2009.

SOURCES FOR QUOTES

p.2   Johannesburg Plan of Implementation 2002, III

p.6   Mathis Wackernagel, Executive Director of Global Footprint Network. http://www.unep.fr/shared/publications/pdf/WEBx0147xPA-Env%20Times%20Newsletter.pdf page 5

p. 8   Pavan Sukhdev, study leader for the project on The Economics of Ecosystems and Biodiversity and the UNEP Green Economy Initiative http://www.unep.fr/shared/publications/pdf/WEBx0147xPA-Env%20Times%20Newsletter.pdf page 6

p. 10   World Economic Forum, http://www.weforum.org/pdf/sustainableconsumption/DrivingSustainableConsumptionreport.pdf page 1

p. 13   Principle 11, Rio Declaration on Environment and Development, 1992.

p. 18   Rink Dickinson, Co-Director, Equal Exchange see: http://www.betterworld.net/quotes/fairtrade-quotes.htm?

p. 21   The business case for sustainability, World Economic Forum, January 2009

p.22   Richard Branson, Founder, Virgin http://www.mjcsustainability.com/

p. 25   Sustainable Consumption Facts and Trends from a Business Perspective, World Business Council for Sustainable Development, 2008

p. 30   WEF, The Global Information Technology Report 2009–2010. http://www.weforum.org/documents/GITR10/index.html. p. v

PHOTOCREDITS

Cover   Left to right: (1) ©Tran Thi Hoa/World Bank, (2) UN Photo/E.Debebe, (3) UN Photo/E.Debebe

p.1   Top left, clockwise: (1) UN Photo/S.Wallace, (2) UN Photo /J.Mohr, (3) UN Photo/E.Debebe

p.2   Top left, clockwise: (1) UN Photo/R.Witlin, (2) UN Photo/J.Issac, (3) World Bank/Y.Hadar

p.3   Top left, clockwise: (1) UN Photo/M.Garten, (2) UN Photo/M.Tzovaras, (3) World Bank/G.Ratushenko

p.5   Top left, clockwise: (1) UN Photo/M.Perret, (2) World Bank/Y.Hadar, (3) UN Photo/F.Kuqi

p.6   UN Photo/M.Perret

p.9   Left, clockwise: (1) UN Photo/E.Debebe, (2) UN Photo/E.Debebe, (3) UN Photo/M.Garten, (4) UN Photo/R.Witlin

p.13   Top left, clockwise: (1) World Bank/A.Gignoux, (2) UN Photo/M.Grant, (3) UN Photo/E.Debebe

p.29   Top left, clockwise: (1) UN Photo/C.Herwig, (2) World Bank/B.Lyons, (3) UN Photo/M.Garten